# Nelson's Children's Minister's Manual

Theresa Plemmons Reiter

## THOMAS NELSON
*Since 1798*

NASHVILLE   DALLAS   MEXICO CITY   RIO DE JANEIRO

Published in Nashville, Tennessee, by Thomas Nelson. Thomas Nelson is a trademark of Thomas Nelson, Inc.

Book design and composition by Upper Case Textual Services, Lawrence, Massachusetts.

Thomas Nelson, Inc., titles may be purchased in bulk for educational, business, fund-raising, or sales promotional use. For information, please e-mail SpecialMarkets@ThomasNelson.com.

**Library of Congress**
  978-1-4185-4496-6 Hardcover

Printed in the United States of America
1 2 3 4 5 6 QG 14 13 12 11

# Contents

# Introduction

I used to consider it an insult when people referred to children's ministry as "glorified babysitting" until I embraced the term and decided to put the "glorified" into the babysitting.

Let's face it, if you are in children's ministry you are dealing with nursery and childcare for worship services, study groups, and church events; however, children's ministry is so much more. Today's children's minister must be a preacher, teacher, babysitter, referee, clown, dance instructor, event planner, counselor, cruise director, caterer, recreation leader, garbage collector, and coach.

Children's ministry requires the patience of Job, the wisdom of Solomon, the endurance of Paul, and the love of Jesus.

It is not for the fainthearted but for the person who has a heart for God and a heart for children. If you have this heart, everything else can be learned. This manual will help you learn the basics, so you can have an effective ministry to children. Some pages will offer gentle reminders of what you already know. Some pages will open your mind and heart to new ideas. My prayer is that every page will be an affirmation of your calling. Do not spend all your time preparing children to be good Christians when they grow up; spend your time helping them be like Christ right now!

Read on.

Prepare to be informed, motivated, challenged, and inspired.

Blessings for the journey,
Theresa Plemmons Reiter

# Chapter 1

## All in a Day's Work

> Teach them to your children, speaking of them
> when you sit in your house, when you walk by the
> way, when you lie down, and when you rise up.
> —Deuteronomy 11:19

Children's ministry is like an airline fare. It is constantly changing. The fact that no two days are the same is what I enjoy most *and* what presents the most frustration. However, although I enjoy the variety and flexibility I often feel frustrated when the day seems chaotic.

### The Typical Atypical Day in Children's Ministry

I meet a member of my children's council for coffee to plan an upcoming event, attend a staff meeting, spray paint pinecones, order T-shirts, decorate a bulletin board, play on the playground with some preschool children, change four diapers, meet with a couple to discuss how they should tell their children they are getting a divorce, and deliver the message for the Wednesday night children's worship. I leave work at the end of a ten-hour day having checked off only three things from the to-do list I prepared the night before. It would seem like an unproductive day, since I completed only three tasks. However, it was one of my most productive days.

A children's ministry program must be organized yet flexible, because ministry often happens in the midst of the interruptions. For example, I was playing with the preschool children on the playground when a child told me about his pet dying the night before. He asked me to pray for him and his family. I told him I would, and he thanked me. Then he said, "I have been standing by the fence hoping you would come, so you would pray for me and give me a hug. I just need it today." Although I did not have "Hug and pray" for the child on my to-do list, it was one of the most meaningful times in my ministry. There is something completely amazing when a child asks you to pray with him or her. A child's faith is so strong and pure. I always consider it such a privilege. It was a great day!

Children's ministry is not just about playing with children. It must be safe, well organized, planned, and theologically sound. Remember, it is not babysitting. You are helping them live their faith today as well as preparing them to be the spiritual leaders of tomorrow. I truly believe this. I see a Mother Teresa, or a Billy Graham, or a Max Lucado in all of them.

How do you balance the play and work aspects of your job? This chapter is going to help with the bare bones of the ministry, give you some great time-saving tools, and get you well on your way to the playground. This chapter alone is worth the price of this book, so pat yourself on the back for your great investment.

There are basic duties in children's ministry that happen no matter the size or denomination of your church.

You must have a child protection policy in place, work with parents, choose curriculum, work with committees or councils, plan special events, refer people in need to various organizations or counseling services, and recruit and train leaders.

Child abuse prevention and ministry protection policies and procedures are essential for all congregations regardless of the size or denomination. We should not only work to protect the safety of our children but also our volunteers and fellow staff. This will be discussed in detail in chapter 7.

# Where to Begin

### Building Relationships with Parents

Believe it or not, children's ministry does not begin with children. Children's ministry actually begins with their parents. You must develop a strong relationship with the parents to have an effective ministry. Partnering with parents is paramount. It is important to realize that they love and know their children better than anyone else.

Spend time getting to know the parents. It is important to observe parents to determine the following: How do they interact with their children? How do they discipline? How do they interact with other children? Are they better with younger or older children? Do they feel grounded in their faith or do they feel they are on the outside looking in? This will help you to better understand their children.

Parents also want to be informed and included. You must always communicate with parents. Help them to understand the overall mission of the ministry and keep them informed of all activities. They should also be involved in the decision-making and planning process. The ministry is not about you but God working through you to help parents and children learn and grow in their faith.

**Create a children's ministry handbook.** The first step in working with parents is to develop a children's ministry handbook. Let them see what the ministry is all about. This handbook should be given to all parents or guardians who have children participating in the ministry at your church. It is also helpful for your church staff to have a copy. Here are some examples of what you may want to include:

- Introduction
  - Introduce yourself and the staff (if applicable)
  - Welcome families to the church
- Contact information
- Purpose of ministry
- Mission statement
- Nursery policies
  - Nursery ages
  - Nursery hours
  - General policies
  - Staff/Volunteer policies
  - Rules

- ○ Illness policies
- ○ Safety polices
- • Sunday school information

  - ○ Classes
  - ○ Age groups
  - ○ Location (including a campus map if necessary)

- • Children's music ministry
- • Any other ministry highlights
- • Security guidelines
- • Check in and check out policies
- • Discipline guidelines
- • Bathroom procedures
- • Child protection policy

---

### Helpful Hint

You may wish to gather handbooks from several churches to help you develop your handbook. Please remember to ask for written permission to copy or use any ideas or logos.

---

## Selecting Curriculum

There are countless catalogs filled with learning resources for children. There are so many it can be difficult to decipher. The first place to begin is with the curriculum published within your denomination.

If you are not satisfied with the curriculum offered, or if you feel you need to supplement your denominational curriculum with other publications, you should first speak with your pastor. Ask if he has a problem with using materials obtained from outside your denomination. If your pastor does not mind your going outside your denomination, ask for recommendations of other materials that may be used. If you are required to stay within your denomination, contact your denomination's publishing company and share your concerns. I did this once within my denomination and was amazed by the response.

If you are open to other teachings and curriculum, take some time to read and explore your options. Many publishing companies will send you samples. You can contact them by phone or e-mail, and this information is usually found on their Web sites. For example, this manual is published by Thomas Nelson. I became familiar with Thomas Nelson many years ago when I received a call asking me if I would be willing to preview some material and see if it would be useful in my ministry. It was a wonderful video series, and I have used it many times throughout my career. I always appreciate the chance to preview new material. Thomas Nelson is a great resource. (I was not compensated in any way for this recommendation.) It is just a little free advice from me to you.

Some examples of programs for which you may need curriculum/study resources are Sunday school, parenting seminars, children's sermons, and retreats, and midweek programs such as Mission Friends, Awana, Pioneer Clubs, and so forth.

## Committees, Councils, Advisory Groups

It may surprise you to know that children's ministry is a team sport. You have to work within the framework of your church as a whole and within the children's ministry area. Staff relationships will be addressed in chapter 2. It is now time to think about how you relate and work with councils, committees, advisory boards, and so on.

If you do not have a children's council, parent group, or advisory board, I would strongly suggest you work within the organizational structure of your church to begin one. This board or council should be either the group of parents or other church members, or both, who help plan and implement all activities and classes for children. They should also be the biggest advocates for the ministry. This group should be made up of people with a strong commitment to Christ and a heart for children's ministry. Since they will be the greatest advocates, they should be people who are trusted and well respected within the congregation. Don't forget to screen all leaders (see chapter 7).

It is most likely you will report to a church board or council. It is important to attend all meetings if possible. The leaders of the congregation need to know you and what is happening in your ministry area. Dress professionally, be on time, and bring your calendar. Be willing to share upcoming events and answer questions.

Pay attention to what is happening in other ministry areas. Seek advice or guidance if needed. Respect others' time and opinions. If your church has a children's council or children's committee that you regularly work with, it is a good idea to have the chairperson attend the meetings with you and give a report on your ministry area.

## Special Events

Children's ministry is full of special events. If you grew up in church there is no doubt your best memories of church will be focused around special events such as vacation Bible school, Easter egg hunts, Christmas pageants, fall festivals, church camps, or revivals.

I love planning special events. In fact, if I were not in ministry I would be an event planner. I realize the love of special event planning is not shared by all who are called into ministry. You may be pleased to know that all of the listed events can be done and done well even if the very thought of an Easter egg hunt for one thousand children gives you hives. The key is to recruit the right leader for the job. Each special event can have a person from your congregation as the director or leader. Look for people who are well organized, excited about the event, and have the time and dedication to make it happen. Once you find the right person you should:

- Give clear expectations of what the event is supposed to achieve.
- Define the success factor.

- Communicate often with your leader/director.
- Work together as a team to develop a list of requirements.
- Decide on a timeline for each requirement to be completed.
- Meet often to stay updated on the progress and offer support or accountability if needed.
- Be a constant cheerleader for the event.

Evaluate each event and make notes to help you if you decide to repeat the event in the future. Don't skip this step! Ask questions such as the following: What did you like most about the event? What would you do differently next year? Of course, the most important question, Are you willing to help with this again if asked? Meet together with key leaders shortly after the event and go over evaluations together. People will have more input if the event is fresh on their minds. Make notes for the next year to help each event improve.

### A Poster Perfect Event

I am a visual person, so I like to make a large poster checklist for each event. This visual reminder serves two purposes: it is a constant reminder of what has to be done, and it is an advertisement to everyone who enters my office of what is needed. People who have viewed the poster have often volunteered to help serve or provide supplies. There is also a great sense of accomplishment when the line beside each item is checked off or the box beside it is filled in. I keep these posters from year to year to remind me that the event can be done.

Here is a sample checklist for a large event:

---

**Name of the event** _____

Budget _____

Date and time requested _____

Check church calendar for conflicts with any other
ministry area _____

Place event on church calendar _____

If this is an outdoor event, what is the rain plan? _____
_____

Do I need to reserve specific space or rooms for
the event? _____

Coordinator _____

Publicity _____

Is food involved? _____

What sort of food? _____

Servers _____

Supplies needed:

_____ , _____ , _____ ,

_____ , _____ , _____ ,

_____ , _____ , _____ ,

_____ .

Setup crew: How many needed and what time? _____

Clean up crew: How many needed and what time? _____

Evaluation complete _____

## Preparing a Reference List

It is important to acknowledge your qualifications and limitations as a children's minister. You may be trained in theology, education, and counseling; however, you are not a trained psychologist or medical doctor. Know your limitations. Act responsibly and professionally.

You should never tell a parent her or his child has ADD, ADHD, or any learning disability or disease if you do not have the credentials to make the diagnosis! It is important to have a reference list of qualified counselors, doctors, psychologists, and psychiatrists you feel comfortable recommending. Check to see if your church has a counselor on staff or a counseling center it supports. Counselors may be members of your congregation or people your pastor(s) or staff recommend. It is also important to decide if your list will only consist of Christian doctors, psychologists, psychiatrists, and so on.

Each time I accept a new church position in an unfamiliar town, I begin the process of establishing a reference list. If no one on the church staff or in the congregation can give me recommendations, I look in the phone book and begin calling psychologists and psychiatrists who specialize in children and families. I tell them I am working to establish a recommendation list for my congregation and would like to take them to lunch to get to know them. I have a list of questions to help me make the decision of whom to recommend. I usually meet with five or six doctors over a period of four or five weeks. I ask questions about their faith, education, what they feel are their specialties, and what they like about their jobs. If I feel good about their responses, I contact their offices and obtain a list of fees and insurances they currently accept. I usually have a list of at least five doctors I can recommend. Each doctor gives me business cards to have available. Doing my homework makes giving the recommendation easy, and every family has been grateful for the fee and insurance information I gathered. In fact, some doctors have been willing to lower or waive fees if needed because of the working relationship we have established. Establishing these relationships with professionals is a great way to provide ministry to hurting families.

It is also important to have a reference list of organizations and Web sites to assist parents in finding help for various disorders, diseases, and disabilities.

### Interview Questions for Psychologists and Psychiatrists

Before you make an appointment with a doctor make sure he or she is accepting new patients!

- Tell me about yourself (education, etc.). (You are looking to see if they are personable, easy to relate to, and easy to understand. Not all doctors are easy to understand.)
- Why did you become a psychologist or psychiatrist? (Are they passionate when they speak of their profession? Do they enjoy what they do?)

- Do you prefer to work with children, adults, or families? Why? (This will help you divide your resource list into three categories: adults, children, families.)
- How do you gauge success in your profession? (Look for doctors who truly want to help people and feel rewarded when families reunite or a child learns coping skills to get through a day of school.)
- What is your faith background? (This is important because you may want to recommend only Christian doctors.)

---

### Helpful Hint

It is important to know that most doctors do not know much about what insurances are accepted at their practices or the various co-pays. It is best to call the office directly and get this information from the insurance specialist.

---

# Chapter 2

## The "His-Functional" Family
### Serving on a Church Staff

There are diversities of gifts, but the same Spirit.
There are differences of ministries, but the same
Lord. And there are diversities of activities, but
it is the same God who works all in all. But the
manifestation of the Spirit is given to each one
for the profit of all: for to one is given the word of
wisdom through the Spirit, to another the word of
knowledge through the same Spirit, to another faith
by the same Spirit, to another gifts of healings by
the same Spirit, to another the working of miracles,
to another prophecy, to another discerning of
spirits, to another different kinds of tongues, to
another the interpretation of tongues. But one and
the same Spirit works all these things, distributing
to each one individually as He wills.

For as the body is one and has many members,
but all the members of that one body, being many,
are one body, so also is Christ. For by one Spirit we
were all baptized into one body—whether Jews or
Greeks, whether slaves or free—and have all been
made to drink into one Spirit. For in fact the body
is not one member but many.

If the foot should say, "Because I am not a hand, I am not of the body," is it therefore not of the body? And if the ear should say, "Because I am not an eye, I am not of the body," is it therefore not of the body? If the whole body were an eye, where would be the hearing? If the whole were hearing, where would be the smelling? But now God has set the members, each one of them, in the body just as He pleased. And if they were all one member, where would the body be?

But now indeed there are many members, yet one body. And the eye cannot say to the hand, "I have no need of you"; nor again the head to the feet, "I have no need of you."

—1 Corinthians 12:4–21

Serving on a church staff is a lot like being in a family. You do not get to choose the members, but you work with who you have. I have served on several church staffs over the past thirty years, and I have to admit some have presented challenges. We all have strengths and gifts, but we all have our imperfections too. It is important to remind yourself that church staffs are made up of imperfect people serving a perfect God in an imperfect world. Let me stress the word *imperfect*. Imperfection is necessary for us to truly understand grace and our need for God. It is important for us to embrace the people on our staffs with the same love, grace, respect, and loyalty we need and expect from them (Matt. 22:37–40; Luke 6:31).

Remember, we are all a part of the body of Christ and no part is more important than another.

My friend Rev. Neil Yongue used to say, "If you see the sausage made, it is difficult to eat the product." This statement is not original to churches, but it definitely does apply. It is a challenge for some to understand that the church must function like a business but remain a spiritual refuge. The church must have personnel policies, budgets, job descriptions, evaluations, performance expectations, and scheduled work hours. The church is also not immune to computer problems, space issues, time constraints, and personality clashes. The larger the staff, the more issues a church can experience. It is important to remember the power of prayer and grace. I currently serve as the director of children's ministries at First United Methodist Church of Lakeland, Florida. There are more than one hundred people on the church's payroll, so you would think there would be constant staff issues and conflicts. This is not the case. We occasionally face difficult issues, but we have several policies and procedures in place to help us work through issues with love, grace, respect, and loyalty.

## Building a Loving, Grace-filled, Respectful, and Loyal Family

At my current church, the first step to building a loving staff-family is how we go about selecting new staff members. It all begins in the hiring process. First UMC Lakeland looks for three Cs in hiring: competence, commitment, and chemistry. Regardless of your church or denomination, these three Cs can form the basis of any interview process.

- Competence: Can the person perform the duties required for the job? Can that candidate do them well? Does the person take pride in his or her job?
- Commitment: Is the person committed to Christ? Is the candidate committed to the mission of the church?
- Chemistry: Will the person be able to establish a working relationship with the current staff and congregation? Will that person be happy at the church, and will she or he work and play well with others?

Once we determine a job applicant has the three Cs, he or she is asked to review our staff behavioral covenant before deciding if he or she wishes to be in ministry with us. The behavioral covenant is written each year with the current staff and states how we plan to work together as a staff. Each staff member signs the covenant as a statement showing his or her willingness to adhere to the covenant.

You may want to establish your own staff behavioral contract. Here are a few suggestions to help you get started.

- Embrace your staff with love, grace, respect, and loyalty.
- Give love, grace, respect, and loyalty in return.
- Pray for every member of your staff.

- Be on time to meetings and come prepared.
- Dress professionally.
- Do not text or take phone calls during meetings. It is important to let the leader of the meeting know if you are expecting a call and that you may need to step out to take a call.
- If you have negative feedback for another staff member, give it privately.
- Be on time to work and keep regular office hours. If you have an administrative assistant, always let that person know your schedule.
- If you are fortunate enough to have an administrative assistant and a maintenance staff, treat them *well*. They are imperative to your ministry.
- Encourage everyone in personal ministries.
- Act on and presume the best motives.
- Listen to others.
- Work to understand one another's responsibilities and time constraints.
- Honor your pastor(s) as servants called by God.
- Affirm one another's gifts.
- Take responsibility for your actions.
- Seek and offer forgiveness.
- Honor confidentiality/avoid gossip.
- Honor the personal time of staff members. Try not to call, text, or e-mail them on their days off or evenings.
- Practice self care. Take your days off, and take time for spiritual growth.

Developing your own covenant in your church will help your staff be a "HIS-functional" family and not a dysfunctional staff. Remember to view successful ministry as God working *through* you. Keep being an open vessel, and keep God in control. This will help you avoid the "proud cloud" as I like to call it. Remember no ministry program can be successful with you alone, and the overall ministry of God's church is your ultimate goal. There is no room for the "proud cloud."

The "proud cloud" is the phrase I use to describe the surroundings of a person who feels his or her ministry area, or even the entire church, could not continue if that person was not there. It is a sense of entitlement. People who are surrounded by the "proud cloud" feel they work harder or have more talent than anyone else on their staff or ministry team. This cloud usually appears after a person has been successful in ministry for a few years or has just completed seminary or divinity school.

---

### Warning!

This cloud contains dangerous levels of arrogance and piety that can harm self and others. This should not be present in a church setting. It is especially dangerous to church staffs. The cloud cannot be used by people who are filled with grace or who give or receive grace. Known side effects of the cloud are alienation of peers, resentment, self-fulfillment over ministry, and in extreme cases loss of appetite for spiritual food or loss of job.

> For by grace you have been saved through faith, and that not of yourselves; it is the gift of God, not of works, lest anyone should boast. For we are His workmanship, created in Christ Jesus for good works, which God prepared beforehand that we should walk in them.
>
> —Ephesians 2:8–10

# Chapter 3

## Keeping the Bar High and the Begging Low
### Recruiting and Training Volunteers

You are not doing anyone a favor from expecting too little from them.

I am sitting in my office on a Monday, and I am flooded with calls and e-mails from people in my congregation begging to be leaders in our children's Sunday school ministry. Sadly, I tell them the positions have been filled for months, but I can put them on a waiting list for the next year. I mention I do have an opening two years out, and if they would like to go online and complete the application, they may do so. They are disappointed about this year but are excited about the possibilities of being a leader in two years. I hang up the phone, turn off my computer, and think to myself, "If only I had enough volunteer positions for every qualified person. It is so difficult to place the chairperson of the religion department at the local university on a waiting list. I just had to. The leadership for fifth grade has been filled for over a year." Then I hear a loud tone and realize my alarm just went off, and I wake up. It was just a dream.

We have all had this dream in one form or another. We have this idea that everyone who feels called to children's

ministry knows their calling and acts on it. We tend to
think making announcements in church where we beg
people to serve or placing a blurb in the Sunday morning
bulletin are enough to motivate people to volunteer for
positions they know very little about. Save your energy
and your paper. Recruiting volunteers is not like searching for a needle in a haystack (which it sometimes feels
like). It is about helping people discover their gifts and
*equipping* them to serve. It is actually my second favorite
part of my job. I love helping people find their place to
serve and then equipping them for the service. The word
equipping may be new to you. It was new to me until I
read the book *The Equipping Church* by Sue Mallory
(Zondervan, 2001). It helped me redefine recruiting and
training as helping people find their gifts, then training
them to use those gifts. There is also a class offered at our
church called "Network." It helps people discover their
gifts. It is great to not only teach the study but also make
the results available to the various ministry areas in your
church. This helps to make recruiting easier for everyone.

## Looking for Subs in All the Wrong Places

A friend of mine, who is a children's director, once
announced from the pulpit on a Sunday morning that
she just needed some warm bodies to be substitute
teachers in Sunday school and to help in the nursery. She
was later frustrated when the volunteers she ended up
with were consistently late and not motivated. When she
asked my opinion on what to do I said, "Well, they were

alive, and that is basically all you asked for." She had set the bar pretty low.

I believe the bar should be set high for volunteers. I have had Dr. Anne Kerr, the President of Florida Southern College teach second grade Sunday school, Reverend Emily Oliver, an ordained Methodist minister who is appointed to our conference office teach second grade Sunday school and Bishop Robert Fannin has served as a greeter and leader for several children's events. Each year several teachers who were voted "teachers of the year" teach vacation Bible school. I am not afraid to ask anyone I feel have the TIPS needed to make them assets in the children's ministry program. (TIPS is an acronym for "trainable," "prayerful," and "servant-hearted.")

## Trainable

Look for people who are open and willing to receive training for the position. In the introduction I said if a person has a heart for God and a heart for children, everything else can be learned. I truly believe this. Training is the key. If a person is willing to be trained in child protection and that person's area of service, then I am willing to provide the best training possible. I love to learn, and I love people who are willing to learn. If a person feels she or he does not need any training and is not willing to be taught our policies and procedures, I do not feel she or he is the right person for our team. Once, I asked the greeters for our Easter egg hunt to attend a training meeting an hour before the event. One of my volunteer greeters was a retired United Methodist bishop. He came to the training on time and eager to learn. I must admit it was quite presumptuous of me to think I could teach a bishop something new, but I was willing to try. When I explained that we had a different way of greeting at children's events than we did at regular church events, I could tell I had his attention. I explained that at children's events we always try to greet children first, then the adults. If the children are small, we will kneel down to speak with them. After the training the bishop said he would have never thought of that. He was and is an amazing advocate for children's ministry in our church.

### Inspirational

Look for people who inspire others with their words and actions.

Children need leaders who have strong relationships with Jesus and are willing to be inspirations to others. These people are well grounded in their faith and have the respect of the congregation. They must also be willing to inspire children to learn and grow in their faith. Inspirational people in your congregation are easy to find. They have attended or led adult Bible studies. They can be motivational but not necessarily outgoing. They can be "gentle giants" who lead quietly and consistently by living their faith or well-respected sports coaches who show their love of Christ though their love of family and friends. My best leaders are people I enjoy being with, and I feel I learn from them.

### Prayerful

Look for people who have a strong faith who communicate with Jesus.

A woman came to me one afternoon with a request. She asked if she could be involved in the children's ministry. As I was reaching for my paper with questions for potential volunteers she told me she did not have children or grandchildren in the program, and she did not really like children or feel comfortable around them. That caught me by surprise. I stopped reaching for my paper and asked why she wanted to help with children's ministry. She said, "Because children are important to God." Well, who can argue with that? We continued to talk about what she enjoyed and what she felt were her spiritual gifts. When she listed prayer as one of her gifts, I knew we needed her on the team.

I do not know where I heard the term "prayer warrior," but I have always wanted a group of prayer warriors to be praying for the children in our church and our community. Organize a prayer group. Discuss how important confidentiality is and develop a covenant not to speak of prayer requests outside the group. Share concerns from the children, upcoming events, and even personal requests with the group. Knowing there are people who pray for you and the children will give you strength and peace in times of need. It will make a tremendous difference in the ministry. Prayer warriors can also be teachers, helpers, childcare providers in the nursery, and event helpers. Those positions are best for those who like children and enjoy being around them.

Pray and seek God's guidance before you ask anyone to serve in a leadership position. Continue to pray for your ministry team throughout their term of service.

Ask how you can pray for them and remind them often that they are being surrounded by prayer.

## Servant-hearted

Look for people who see themselves as serving others, not themselves.

I am going to share with you a huge secret that veteran children and youth directors have been keeping for years. We usually let people find out on their own the hard way, but I am going to let you in on the secret: All volunteers do not have the heart of a servant, and some can be difficult to work with. Yep, I said it. I have thought it for years, but I do not know if I have ever actually had the nerve to say it out loud. It is true, and it is a challenge. You can avoid dealing with challenging volunteers if you recruit people to be on the ministry team who have the heart of a servant. This means they are willing to see their positions as serving others, not themselves. Some people want to work with children because they want to be children again, some want to play but not have responsibilities, some want to make sure the ministry goes the way they want it to go. They usually have their own agendas that are not compatible with the mission of the ministry.

You can usually tell if a person has the heart of a servant by the answers the person gives to the list of interview guidelines for employees and volunteers found on pages 48–52. Carefully consider the answers to the questions dealing with forgiveness and working within a group or team. People who have the heart of a servant are willing to give and accept forgiveness, and work with a group or team. They are open to new ideas and do not mind if they have a title or receive recognition. The success of the ministry serves as their recognition.

Servant-hearted volunteers are like precious jewels to any leader. They are the most valuable volunteers, and you should cherish them. Surround yourself with these people and consistently let them know how valuable they are. They may not *need* to hear it but they will *appreciate* hearing it.

## Working for TIPS or How Do You Get the Best Volunteers

Now that you know the type of people you are looking for, you must establish your volunteer needs and begin recruiting. Remember, I am a visual person, so I make a table. I do not usually put this one in poster form (yet). The chart basically lists the position to be filled, qualifications/expectations, a list of people who qualify for the position, and who accepts the position.

| Position | Qualifications/Expectations | Candidates | Filled by |
|---|---|---|---|
|  |  |  |  |
|  |  |  |  |
|  |  |  |  |
|  |  |  |  |
|  |  |  |  |

Volunteer positions range from long-term commitments such as Sunday school team members and Wednesday night leaders to short-term commitments such as servers for the Fall Festival.

If you are working with a ministry leadership team, a council, or even your church staff, it is good to include them in this process of developing a list of potential volunteers. It is wonderful to have either a group of people or your pastor(s), or both, to help you brainstorm about potential volunteers for everything from teaching to face painting.

After you have completed your chart and have possible candidates lined up for each position, work together as a team to rank the candidates in order beginning with who the group feels is the best choice for the position. Then the real work begins. It is the part most children's ministry leaders dread the most: obtaining volunteers.

## The Dreaded Phone Call

I have friends in children's ministry who get physically sick when they have to make phone calls to recruit volunteers. The fear of rejection is just overwhelming. The source of frustration and fear comes from the misconception of *why* we are calling. We feel like we are making a sales call or calling from a charity to ask for a donation. We then feel rejected when someone says no. That is not what we are doing. We are not selling God or begging people to give to God. We are calling to offer a service to them.

We are offering to help them discover and use their God-given spiritual gifts. When a person says no it is usually because he or she has time constraints, does not feel it is a personal gift, or has never considered serving. Those are all great reasons. If volunteering is going to become a burden to someone I certainly do not want that person to accept. If a person is uncomfortable with the position, feels overwhelmed by the task, and does not feel training will help, then God will use him or her in another way.

If a person has never considered serving and sees church as an hour-a-week commitment, then I have opened the door for him or her to think about service. Every phone call or conversation has a purpose whether the person accepts or not. The reason I have included the word *conversation* in addition to the phone call is because it is always better to ask in person. Take him or her to coffee or invite him or her on a walk. Always be excited about the ministry. No one wants to feel like he or she is boarding a sinking ship, but everyone does like to be asked to join a group when an enthusiastic leader asks. Remember when you were a child and people were choosing teams? Everyone likes the feeling of being the first person chosen. Never use the phrase "last resort" or say you have no one else to ask. People often say to me they will take a position if I do not find anyone else. I reply by saying, "I do not want anyone else. You are my first choice." It does not always work but sometimes it does.

# Training Those Trainable, Inspirational, Prayerful, Servant-hearted People

When people are given jobs they want to know the purpose, responsibilities, and what resources are available to help them serve in the best way possible. Training should be fun, informative, and productive. People need to leave training feeling like it was worth their time. It only takes one bad training class to make people never attend another one. This is not an exaggeration. I once served at a church for five years, and even in year five people were still talking about the boring Sunday school leader training sessions they were made to attend two years before I began working there. They simply refused to ever come to another training event.

### The Meal

I consider training a meal. There should be an appetizer, meat, side dish, and dessert.

**The Appetizer.** The appetizer *is* actually food. Every volunteer training event begins with food. That is my appetizer. It may be a snack, brunch, lunch, or dinner. It does not have to be expensive or extravagant, but being creative never hurts. You can choose a theme or just a theme color. Who would not like to attend a fiesta-themed training session with a piñata filled with candy, gift cards, jewelry, and small toys to use in class? I once did this and was a little frightened by how much the Sunday school leaders loved beating something with a stick. The training was talked about for years, and training sessions were always well attended.

**The Meat.** The meat is the core of the training. Give them what they need! Everyone should receive a job description with her or his purpose and responsibilities—as well as expectations—listed. Each person should be given curriculum if applicable, and access to all resources needed to serve in her or his position. For example, if you are training Sunday school leaders you would give them class lists with contact information, tours of their classrooms, curriculum, teacher guides, child protection policies, and age group characteristics, and show them where to find supplies such as construction paper, glue, and scissors. If you are training for vacation Bible school you would present the theme, introduce curriculum, list the schedule, and so on. All volunteers who work directly with children should receive child protection training as well as training in age-appropriate discipline. This would be the meat of the training.

**The Side Dish.** The side dish would be additional resources offered to anyone who may want them. A resource table filled with Bible maps, devotional books, Bible dictionaries, posters, and so forth is always appreciated at a Sunday school or vacation Bible school training session.

**The Dessert.** The dessert is the theme, decorations, or the fun part of the event. It can be as simple as placing a dot on the back of one chair and giving a door prize to the person who sits there or decorating the entire room in a theme complete with music and costumes. You can be as creative as you wish with your training, but make sure your focus does not get lost in the theme.

Always invite your pastor(s) to attend or participate in volunteer training. If you are not comfortable training volunteers, your pastor(s) may be willing to provide the training or help you find a qualified person to lead.

Provide evaluations for participants to fill out listing ways future trainings could be improved.

Here are a few job description samples and age-level learning characteristics you may use to help train your leaders:

## Job Description: Teacher

The purpose of your role is to plan and implement weekly lessons that will provide each child with an opportunity to learn and grow in faith and to nurture each child so that she or he will experience the love of Christ through you.

*Your Responsibilities Are To:*

- Read the curriculum and prepare the lesson.
- Verify that the required supplies and resources will be available by contacting the education office early in the week.
- Arrive before the children (by _____ a.m./p.m.) to arrange the class as you wish and to discuss any ways in which the secretary and helper can assist you.
- Ensure that the guidelines of the child protection policy are met and request help from the education office if necessary to remain within these guidelines.
- If you are unable to attend on your scheduled Sunday, please contact a substitute as soon as possible and let us know who will be teaching your class.
- Show the love of Christ to each child in your class.

*Sunday Morning Contacts and Information:*

Name _____

Phone/Cell _____

Location of supply closet if applicable _____

_____

_____

## Job Description: Helper/Assistant

The purpose of your role is to assist the Sunday school teacher in the ways that best serve both the teacher and students. You are the extra eyes, ears, and hands for our teachers.

*Your Responsibilities Are To:*

- Arrive to class no later than _____ a.m./p.m. to discuss any specific help the teacher may need for that day.
- Greet parents and children as they sign in. Remember to always greet the children first.
- Provide support by passing out and collecting supplies as needed.
- Assist children with crafts, activities, etc.
- Walk children to the restroom if requested (never allow them to go unaccompanied by a screened adult).
- Contact _____ if additional supplies or helpers are needed.
- If you are unable to attend on your scheduled Sunday, please contact a substitute as soon as possible and let us know who will be helping in your class.
- Show the love of Christ to each child in your class.

*Sunday Morning Contacts:*

Name _____

Phone/Cell _____

## Job Description: Secretary

The purpose of your role is to support the Sunday school teacher by providing assistance during sign-in time; sending notes to children for birthdays, special events, and missed Sundays; and calling and reminding parent volunteers.

*Your Responsibilities Are To:*

- Arrive by _____ a.m./p.m.
- Greet parents and children as they enter the room. Remember to always greet the children first.
- Assist parents and children with the sign-in process, ensuring that each parent in Nursery 2 through Grade 5 indicate (by name) *who* will be picking up her or his child.
- Give children stickers to place beside their names on the attendance chart.
- Follow the instructions listed in the Sunday school binder.
- Ensure that the guidelines of the child protection policy are met and request help from the the education office if necessary to remain within these guidelines.
- If you are unable to attend on your scheduled Sunday, please contact a substitute as soon as possible and let us know who will be serving in your place.
- Show the love of Christ to each child in your class.

*Sunday Morning Contacts:*

To request help or supplies, contact _____

_____

Phone/Cell  _____

| Ways to Help Children Grow in Their Faith at Any Age | | |
| --- | --- | --- |
| Age | Building a Foundation | Learn and Respond |
| Infant/ Toddler | • Have an inviting atmosphere. It should be safe, with age-appropriate toys, books, and music.<br>• They should be shown love even through separation, anxiety, sharing, and potty challenges.<br>• They need patient, loving adults willing to offer gentle guidance in how to respect rights of others and in how to be friends. | • See the Bible as a special book.<br>• Hear Bible stories and show pictures.<br>• Show pictures of Jesus, Adam and Eve, Moses, and Noah. |
| Ages 3–5 (preschool) | • Guide children in activities that help them play with others.<br>• Provide optional activities for decision making. Help them feel loved and accepted unconditionally.<br>• Have good adults who can provide positive behaviors for children to imitate.<br>• Include appropriate music with simple language they can repeat and understand. | • Children need to see the Bible being used.<br>• Read stories aloud from the Bible.<br>• Begin to teach faith traditions.<br>• Introduce them to the Lord's Prayer. |

| Age | Building a Foundation | Learn and Respond |
|---|---|---|
| Ages 6–8 | • Offer several activities for children to choose from.<br>• Provide group and individual activities.<br>• Encourage children to bring their own Bibles (this may be a great time to give children Bibles).<br>• Help children understand and participate in worship.<br>• Share stories of how people shared their faith in the Bible and how they can share their faith with others. | • Encourage children to read the Bible at church and home.<br>• Teach and encourage children to have a daily devotion time.<br>• Teach how the Bible came to us.<br>• Teach sacraments.<br>• Teach children to use study helps in their lessons such as maps, table of contents, concordance, etc.<br>• Explain division of Old and New Testaments.<br>• Help children locate Scripture in the Bible. |
| Ages 9–12 | • Explore ways for children to participate in mission projects.<br>• Teach basics of denominational beliefs and practices.<br>• Explore various forms of worship.<br>• Teach responsibility for faith.<br>• Encourage children to interpret Scripture. | • Help children to memorize Scripture.<br>• Learn denominational vocabulary.<br>• Focus on putting Bible knowledge into practice.<br>• Understand divisions in the Bible.<br>• Introduce them to other Christian writings. |

# Interview Guidelines for Employees and Volunteers

There are a number of interview questions that can help determine the motives behind why people want to work or volunteer with children. Ask these questions and keep notes to help you in the volunteer and/or employment process.

- Tell me about yourself. (This begins the interview with a nonthreatening, open-ended question.)
- Summarize your employment history. (Look for frequent moves, gaps in employment, and reasons for termination. If you are looking for a reliable volunteer or employee, this question will give you valuable information.)
- Tell me about your experience with children. Have you worked or volunteered for other children or youth organizations? (Watch for adults whose lives seem to revolve around spending time with children.)
- What strengths can you bring to this job or position?
- Why do you want to work with children? (Watch to see if the candidate is too child focused or wants to work with children because they are "pure," "innocent," "trusting," "nonjudgmental," "clean," and so on. Adults

should want to work with children because
they have something to offer children. Be aware
of the adults who want to work with children
because children meet adult needs.)

- What do you do in your spare/leisure time? Tell
  me about your hobbies or interests. (Watch for
  people who want to spend their free time with
  children and hobbies that are more appealing
  to children than adults. For example, video
  games, puzzles, magic, models, and so forth. It
  is okay for an adult to enjoy playing games with
  children but adults should have adult friends
  and participate in adult activities. If a person
  is immersed in the world of children it may be
  because she or he has not reached the maturity
  level of an adult. This may be due to fear. It
  is important to offer the person ways to grow
  in her or his faith with other adults and build
  adult relationships.)

- What ages of children do you prefer to work
  with? (Watch for a candidate who only wants
  to work with a specific age. It is okay for
  people to have a preference but listen carefully
  if a person *only* wants to work with one age
  group. A negative example of this might be:
  "I like working with the little ones because
  I can 'control' them." It is never good to put
  someone in a leadership position who is
  seeking control. Listen for continual "I want" or
  "I need" statements. You want volunteers who

are focused on the needs of children, not their own needs. Challenge the person to step out of his or her comfort zone and teach another age group. See if the person is open to seeing a personal gift within that he or she may not have recognized before or if the person shuts down because of not getting his or her way.)

- Do you have any reservations about working with children of different ages? (It is okay if candidates have reservations. The important thing here is listening to see if they are willing to express their reservations or if they get nervous when you ask the question. People who are comfortable with themselves are able to admit what challenges them.)

- Do you think there are any reasons to treat boys and girls differently? (Listen closely to their responses and rationale. Do the answers feel right?)

- How were you disciplined as a child? Do you feel the discipline was appropriate? (Note if the family resolved problems by physical punishment.)

- What do you consider acceptable discipline? (Avoid adults who need control.)

- How do you deal with stress? (Look for positive outlets for stress such as exercise, scrapbooking, or taking time out for themselves. Be aware of people who say they do not have stress or they punch walls. [I actually had someone tell me this once.] You do not want anyone to ever use violence to handle stress.)

- What is your plan for dealing with stress?
- What makes you angry? (Avoid people who cannot admit they have been angry. Look for people to be real. However, if they can immediately give you long lists of things that make them angry, you will most likely be on those lists soon.)

---

**RED FLAG!**

Beware if someone says, "I don't like people telling me how to do my job or correcting me" or "I love children but their parents drive me crazy." People who lead children must be able to relate to parents.

---

- If you saw another teacher/staff/volunteer—one whom you like and respect—strike a child, what would you do? (Make sure at some point the candidate plans to tell a supervisor.)
- Have you ever been reprimanded at work? For what? (Was the person's reprimand related to dealing with children?)
- Who are your best friends? (Adults' best friends should be other adults.)

- Do you relate better with children or adults? (Be cautious of anyone who relates better to children than adults.)
- How do you feel you can best serve the children of our congregation and community?
- Do you like working within a group or alone?
- Can you share examples of when you have given and when you have received forgiveness?

## Sample Forms

### Evaluation Form

Name of the Event _____ Date _____

What did you enjoy most? _____

_____

_____

_____

What did you find to be the most challenging? _____

_____

_____

_____

What would you change next year? _____

_____

_____

_____

You can do a rating system and list different elements of the event such as:

---

Rate each part of the retreat from 1 through 10, with 1 being the lowest rating and 10 being the highest rating.

Music _____ Small-group time _____ Session 1 _____

Worship _____ Schedule _____

Food: Breakfast _____ Lunch _____ Dinner _____

Communication: Church _____ Community _____

Name (optional) _____

May we contact you to be on the planning or leadership team for this event next year? (name, e-mail address, and phone number required) _____

_____

---

# Chapter 4

## Herding Sheep with a Feather
### Dealing with Discipline

But Jesus said, "Let the little children come to Me, and do not forbid them; for of such is the kingdom of heaven.

—Matthew 19:14

A church's discipline policy can be a challenge because it is different from a daycare or school policy, or the type of discipline used in one's home. It is important to set clear expectations, use positive language and reinforcements, and always rule on the side of grace. Forgive, forget, and let each week be a new beginning for each child.

Entire books are written dealing with discipline alone. Some books I would recommend are *The Discipline Guide for Children's Ministry* by Jody Capehart, Gordon West, and Becki West (Group Publishing, 1997), the *Pocket Guide to Discipline: Quick Tips for a Stress-Free Classroom* by Gordon West and Becki West (Group Publishing, 2006), the *Pocket Guide to Discipline* by Group Publishing (Group Publishing, 2006), and the *Pocket Guide to Special Needs* by Group Publishing (Group Publishing, 2008).

Here are some brief tips to get you started on the right track.

1. Be prepared

   The tone for an event is set by the organization or disorganization in the room the second the child enters. The room should be set up, activities should be ready, the greeter should be in place, and children need to be recognized by name. Name tags are essential! Children are most likely to present discipline challenges when they are bored, overlooked, overwhelmed, or frustrated. All these things can be easily avoided if you are prepared.

2. Give Clear and Defined Instructions Using Words Children Will Understand

   Use positive language to express what you would like him or her to do rather than negative language expressing your desire to have the child stop what he or she is doing. Here are some examples.

   • A child is running down the sidewalk.

     ◦ Positive: "Walk please. We need to be safe."
     ◦ Negative: "Stop running."

   • A child is consistently talking during a project.

- ○ Positive: "Please work quietly on your puzzle so you can help others concentrate."
  - ○ Negative: "Stop talking."
- A child is dripping paint over the table.
  - ○ Positive: "Let's work to keep the paint on our papers so we can have nice tables in our classrooms."
  - ○ Negative: "You are making a mess."

3. Kindness matters

   Yelling, belittling, humiliating, embarrassing, and making comparisons to other children are not acceptable. One can be firm but kind, stern yet fair, and controlled but flexible. It sounds impossible but it can be done!

4. Let Your Class or Small Groups Develop Rules for the Group

   Begin each rule with positive words. Make a poster and let each child add his or her handprint, fingerprint, and name, so they all have ownership of the rules and feel accountable. Fingerprints, handprints, or names can be added by new children as they join.

- We will listen to and respect our teacher.
- We will be kind to one another.
- We will take care of our classroom and supplies.

- We will participate in the activities.
- We will ask for forgiveness and forgive.
- We will pray for one another.

It may be helpful to use the rules in disciplining a child. For example, call a child aside and speak in a low voice. We never want to embarrass, call out, or humiliate. Say, "Alex, you placed your handprint on the poster saying you would listen to the teacher. Can you show me your handprint (name, etc.)?" When the child shows you the handprint (or name, etc.), say, "Yes, there it is. I knew you just needed a reminder. Thank you." This is a great activity for your teaching assistant.

5. Get to know children

Find out their hobbies and interests. If they are not interested in the lesson or activity work, relate the lesson or activity to their interests.

For example, you have a child in your kindergarten class who loves *Star Wars*. You are teaching the story of Noah's ark. The child is not interested and would rather walk around the room than sit in the story circle.

You call him over and tell him you are Yoda, and you need him to be Luke Skywalker, and that you are going to train him to help you teach this lesson. You may even want to roll up a piece of paper to be a light saber. Together you tell the story. Be sure to thank him for being such a great storyteller, and remind him he served God in a special way by letting all the children in the classroom hear God's message. You may want to send him a follow-up note in the mail. Children love to receive mail.

6. Be consistent with praise and discipline.

7. Choose your words carefully and follow through if you have said there will be consequences for an action.

8. Maintain control but understand the definition of control changes according to the age group.

9. Understand age-level characteristics that help children build a spiritual foundation, learn, and respond. Refer to the guide on pages 46–47 of this manual.

10. Be familiar with learning disabilities or illnesses that can affect a child's learning.

These behaviors can sometimes be viewed as discipline problems when they are not. The child may need to learn a different way. Never underestimate the power of prayer. Pray for the children in your ministry. Refer to resource guide on pages 55 and 100–102 of this manual.

# Chapter 5

## Caring for Little Ones Is a Big Job
### Providing Quality Childcare Is
### Just the Beginning

But Jesus said, "Let the little children come to Me,
and do not forbid them; for of such is the kingdom
of heaven."

—Matthew 19:14

I once heard a story about a man who said he did not
attend church because he flunked out of church. She was
very surprised to hear such a story because she was not
aware that one could flunk out of church.

She asked him how this was possible, and he said
he attended catechism class. When he completed the
class he was expected to be able to answer certain questions. He said he answered the first question wrong and
flunked. Of course she was quite curious so she asked,
"What was the question?"

He said he was asked, "Who was the first to see Jesus
when he arose from the dead?" She did wonder how anyone
could miss such an easy question. After all, there are several answers that would be true. One could say Mary, Mary
Magdalene, Peter, or John. How did he miss it? When she
asked him what his answer was, he said, "I think the first to
see Jesus alive were the tiny spiders in the tomb."

This story totally caught me by surprise. It made me rethink how I viewed the ministry of our church nursery. I have always been dedicated to making our church nursery the safest, cleanest, most aesthetically pleasing, and most comfortable place for parents/guardians to leave their children, so they could attend worship, Bible studies, or meetings. Childcare providers are background screened, trained in nursery procedures, CPR, and child protection policies. Our toys are safe and age appropriate, we have a strict sign-in/sign-out policy, and we issue pagers to parents so they can be summoned if needed. I thought we were doing everything right until I heard a story about who was the first to see Jesus after he arose from the tomb. It made me realize I was not doing enough for the children. I was making the nursery about the parents. The part of the story that enlightened me about ministry in the nursery was the man's comment that the first to see the living Jesus were "the tiny spiders." That resonated with me. I could not help thinking we have been so busy making the nursery about the parents that we have forgotten how the smallest spiders are seeing the living Christ (I apologize for comparing sweet babies to tiny spiders), but bear with me. The church nursery is more than daycare, mom's morning out, or a play group. It is truly the first place children come in contact with the living Christ. It is a ministry. It is *not* babysitting.

# The Setting

We have already addressed how the nursery should be safe, easy for parents to find, and aesthetically pleasing, but the church nursery needs more than just a mural of Noah's ark to make it a ministry. Nursery ministry should be intentional. Age-appropriate Christian music, books, and pictures should be used. Bulletin boards should include pictures of Jesus and other Bible characters. If you share space with the preschool you may need to gently remind its leaders that the church is a church first, and the church is being used as a preschool. Faith pictures need to be displayed.

Childcare providers should read stories of Jesus loving others, Jesus feeding people, and Jesus helping others. It is never too early to begin reading to children. I believe children are the closest to God we can see on earth. In the book *Between the Dreaming and the Coming True: The Road Home to God* (Tarcher, 2001), Robert Benson tells the story of a four-year-old girl who was overheard whispering into her newborn baby brother's ear, "'Baby,' she whispers, 'tell me what God sounds like. I'm starting to forget.'" (55)

We simply cannot forget how precious children are to God and how the church nursery is our first opportunity for them to see and experience the living Christ.

# How to Have the Best Possible Church Nursery

There are a few things you can do to make your church nursery the best it can be. It all starts with the best people and a list of strong, clear policies and procedures.

1. Hire the best people and recruit the very best volunteers. Look for loving, nurturing, responsible people who have a healthy self-esteem.

2. Nursery workers should be called "caregivers."

3. Caregivers should be background screened and provide references, and those references should be checked and documented by a designated staff member. Caregivers should be trained in first aid, infant and child CPR, and nursery policies. There are several ways to get your workers trained in age-appropriate CPR. The most cost-effective way is to search for a member of your church who is certified to teach. Ask him or her if he or she is willing to lead training for free or for just the cost of the supplies. You can also call your local fire department and request training, contact local preschools to see if you can bring workers to their training, or check hospital schedules for trainings. There is usually a cost associated with the training, and churches pay for

training their employees. If you have nursery volunteers or cannot afford to pay for training, you can ask members of the congregation to sponsor a worker. You might be surprised how many people will help when the safety of children is involved.

4. Provide a safe, clean, age-appropriate environment, with age-appropriate toys.

5. There should be room for toddlers to roam around the room safely.

6. A check-in/checkout policy should be clearly written and understood by staff that will be responsible for making sure parents understand the check-in/check-out policy.

7. There should be space available for children's bags. Bags should be properly marked and contain diapers, wipes, formula, and snacks.

8. If there are children with allergies, mark them with a bold-colored sticker. They will feel special and you will keep them safe.

9. Create a diaper-changing procedure and post it so everyone can follow it.

## Helpful Handouts

Here are some basic handouts to help you recruit and train nursery caregivers (volunteer and staff).

## Expectations

- Childcare providers should pray for the children entrusted in their care.

- Everyone should know the mission of the church nursery. Work together with the staff and volunteers to establish expectations.

- Relay how important it is for childcare givers to arrive on time.

- Photo name badges are a great way to tell parents who are screened workers.

- Every child's diaper should be changed just before the child is picked up.

- Children who are potty training should try to go to the bathroom during their nursery stay at least once. (Never scold for accidents.)

- Clean and straighten the room after each use. Disinfect toys after each use.

## Interaction with Parents

- Always thank parents for bringing their children, and remind them it is a pleasure to spend time with their children.
- Always smile (even if you are tired or frazzled).
- Share with parents any diaper or feeding event.
- Follow dismissal procedures.
- Try to say something positive about each child to the child's parent.

## Teachable Moments

Talk to the child while you are changing her or his diaper. Explain what you are doing, and use the child's name often. You may also sing to the child while changing her or his diaper or clothes.

Help children share toys. This is not natural to children. They must learn this behavior. You can be a great role model to follow.

## Discipline

Always use a kind voice. If children hit, bite, or shove, remove them from the situation. Remind them we do not hit, bite, or shove our friends. End with a positive remark like, "We are kind to our friends."

## Age-Group Characteristics

Please note babies and toddlers develop at different stages. This does not indicate a child is underdeveloped or slow. Do not compare babies at this age because development variations are so prevalent.

### Birth to Six Weeks

Babies are sleepy most of the time. They begin to recognize their parents and listen to human voices. They have very limited control of their bodies. They also can be startled by loud noises or sharp sounds.

### Six Weeks to Three Months

Babies may show real interest in their surroundings. They are becoming stronger and more coordinated with their hands. They are beginning to smile, and they enjoy looking into people's faces. They can begin tracking objects.

## Three Months to Five and a Half Months

Babies respond to new voices and may finger objects with both hands. They like to bring objects to their mouths. They enjoy kicking. They gain head control in an upright position and are learning to reach. They can become sensitive to sounds, words, and voices. They may also laugh out loud.

## Five and a Half Months to Eight Months

Babies may turn over or sit up. They enjoy being upright. They usually are not happy around strangers and are very curious about their surroundings. They can usually clap hands, attempt to crawl, bat at objects, and begin to solve problems.

## Eight Months to Twelve Months

Babies may crawl or even walk. They are beginning to understand language and develop fine motor skills. They love to explore and try to imitate and mimic.

## Toddler Trauma

Toddlers are going through so many changes during this time. They can be happy one moment and frustrated the next. They want to be independent and try things themselves. However, they will try things they may not be ready for. Here are a few things that help ease toddler trauma:

- Understand frustrations. Toddlers want to perform activities they are not yet capable of.

- Be patient with children. Demonstrate new skills, and move at the child's pace.

- Enjoy playing with the children. Learn together.

- Interact with the children. Get on their eye level. Sit on the floor.

## Basic Diaper-Changing Procedures

1. Gather necessary supplies.
2. Clean diaper-changing surface.
3. Wash your hands.
4. Cover diaper-changing area with clean paper.
5. Put on disposable gloves (avoid latex because of possible children's allergies).
6. Place the child on diapering surface.
7. Remove the soiled diaper.
8. Clean the child's diaper area thoroughly with disposable wipes.
9. Dispose of the diaper properly. (Place the cloth diaper in a plastic bag, or secure the disposable diaper by folding it inward, placing it in plastic-lined container, and closing the lid.)
10. Remove and dispose of the gloves.
11. Put a clean diaper on the child.
12. Use a separate cloth to clean the child's hands and face.
13. Remove the child from the diaper area.
14. Clean the diaper-changing area.
15. Clean the diaper-changing surface.
16. Return all supplies to the proper storage area.
17. *Wash your hands!*

## Communication

In addition to handouts for volunteers and staff, you should also prepare a brochure to give to all the parents. Communication is key.

Include:

- purpose;
- nursery hours;
- general policies, such as "Bring a bag for each child with the child's name marked on it," etc.;
- ages of children for whom care is provided;
- nursery rules, such as illness policies, rules for parent volunteers, etc.;
- safety points, such as sign-in and signout policies, why you issue pagers, identification for staff and volunteers, etc.; and
- potty policies, why changes of clothes are needed, etc.

You may want to include contact information and titles of staff members, and a list of parenting help books or resources for child development.

# Chapter 6

## Denomination Station

> Then he said, "The God of our fathers has chosen
> you that you should know His will, and see the Just
> One, and hear the voice of His mouth."
>
> —Acts 22:14

It is a common belief that all mainstream denominations are the same, and it is easy to change denominations as a children's minister or director of children's ministry. It is not quite as easy as one would think. It requires a great deal of prayer, thought, and research.

### Understanding the Denomination

I grew up in a Baptist church and attended both a Presbyterian and a Baptist college. I have served on staff in three different denominations. Some transitions were easier than others. I did not notice the differences as much while serving churches as a college student, but when I became a full-time staff member the challenges were more prevalent. This does not mean any one denomination is better than another. They all have wonderful ministries, and I have been blessed by every church I served, but there are some significant differences.

First of all, denominations have their own language—okay, maybe not their own language, but they do have different vocabularies. I remember my first week serving as the youth director at the First United Methodist Church of Hendersonville, North Carolina. I had been in ministry for more than seven years in the Baptist denomination. I wanted to move to my hometown and found out about the church position from a friend in the chaplaincy department at the local hospital. She said it was a wonderful church with wonderful ministries throughout the community. I met with a Methodist minister in the town where I was currently serving to discuss theological differences and similarities. I felt comfortable with the change and, after applying, was granted an interview. The interview focused on personality, qualifications, and ability to relate to teenagers. It was a wonderful interview; I was elated to receive the job offer, and I was thrilled to accept.

The challenges came my first week on the job. I was in a meeting with my adult council and this question was asked: "What do you have planned for UMYF?" I was totally thrown by the question. I had no idea what UMYF was. I sat in silence trying to think what UMYF could possibly be an acronym for. Then someone asked, "What do you have planned for Sunday-night youth?" I was then told UMYF was an acronym for United Methodist Youth Fellowship. This is what United Methodists called their Sunday-night youth ministries at the time. Oh, I had a plan; I just did not know what I had a plan for. I was fortunate to be a part of a council who was not only willing to laugh about the misunderstanding but to offer forgiveness and give me guidance on United Methodist beliefs and policies.

I would like to say this was my only mistake in my newfound denomination, but it was not. There were many more "learning opportunities." Here are a few new definitions I learned in my first few months: social principles, *The Discipline,* bishop, prevenient grace, infant baptism, administrative board, Council on Ministries, pledging, Staff-Parish Relations Committee, YSF (Youth Service Fund), UMCOR (United Methodist Committee on Relief), and district superintendent. This is a very short list of new vocabulary I had to learn and use.

I will be eternally grateful for Dr. Doug Kilgo, the chairperson of the Staff-Parish Relations Committee, who hired me and to Dr. Susanne Kilgo, who served as the youth coordinator at First United Methodist Church. They patiently taught me the policies and procedures in The United Methodist Church. The adult council who planned and implemented all youth events was instrumental in helping me gain a clear understanding of The United Methodist Church. They introduced me to The United Methodist Publishing House and curricula. I served happily at First United Methodist Church for many years. I will always be grateful for the many opportunities I was given to learn and grow in my faith and knowledge.

The key to my happy transition was the willingness of the people to help me learn and grow. If you plan on changing denominations you must first share core theological beliefs with the denomination that you are considering. Review your current pension plan because it will most likely not transfer. You may want to consult with an accountant. Be prepared for a change in your status. No, I am not talking about your Facebook status. You may now be a leader within your current denomination. Maybe you have written curriculum, been a speaker at events, or served on denominational committees. These things do not carry over. You will most likely have to reestablish yourself in these areas.

It is also important to ask during the interview process if you could have a mentor to help you understand the organizational differences as well as the theological differences. Ask the interviewer to help you find the right person in the congregation to help mentor you and help you on your journey.

It is also helpful to know the names of the various publishing companies associated with specific denominations.

# Denominational Publishing Companies

**Assemblies of God**
    Gospel Publishing House

**Baptist**
    **American Baptist Churches, USA**
    Judson Press

    **Baptist Missionary Association of America**
    Baptist Publishing House

**Southern Baptist Convention**
Lifeway Christian Resources

**Unaffiliated**
Smyth & Helwys

**Christian Church (Disciples of Christ)**
Christian Board of Publication

**Christian Reformed Church**
CRC Publications

**Church of God**
Warner Press

**Episcopal Church**
Church Publishing
Cowley Publications
Forward Movement
Leader Resources

**Lutheran**
**Evangelical Lutheran Church in America**
Augsburg Fortress Publishers

**The Lutheran Church-Missouri Synod**
Concordia Publishing House

**Mennonite Church**
Faith and Life Press
Herald Press

**Nazarene**
    Beacon Hill Press

**Nondenominational/Mainstream Christian**
    Thomas Nelson Publishing
    Group Publishing

**Presbyterian Church**
    **Cumberland Presbyterian Church**
    Board of Christian Education

    **Presbyterian Church in America**
    Great Commission Publications

    **Presbyterian Church (U.S.A.)**
    Bridge Resources
    Curriculum Publishing
    Presbyterian Publishing House
    Witherspoon Press

**United Methodist Church**
    Cokesbury
    Upper Room
    Abingdon Press

**United Church of Christ**
    Pilgrim Press
    United Church Press

# Chapter 7

## We Are Called to Serve and Protect
### Child Protection Policies

God is my strength and power, and He makes my way perfect.

—2 Samuel 22:33

A great deal of this manual is devoted to keeping children safe in your church. It is a sad reality that much time and energy must be devoted to this task. If you choose to read any one chapter of this manual, choose this chapter.

The Florida United Methodist Conference offers a child protection policy template for United Methodist churches in Florida. It includes requirements and guidelines for churches to use in creating their own policies. It is important for all churches to implement policies and adopt procedures to protect children and recognize that our Christian faith calls us to offer both hospitality and protection to the children. The social principles of The United Methodist Church state that "children must be protected from economic, physical, and sexual exploitation and abuse" (*The Book of Resolutions of The United Methodist Church*, 2008, §162C). Tragically, churches have not always been safe places for children.

Child sexual abuse and exploitation occur in churches both large and small, urban and rural. The problem cuts across all economic, cultural, and racial lines. God calls us to make our churches safe places, protecting children and other vulnerable persons from abuse.

It is important that every church have child protection policies and procedures in place to keep children safe, and procedures in place for reporting abuse. Carefully selecting staff /volunteers and properly supervising them is the key to child/youth safety. More injuries, claims, and lawsuits emanate from improper supervision than from any other reason, including using unsafe facilities. Focus on supervision.

## How to Develop a Child Protection Policy

Check with your denomination headquarters to see if there is a template or policy to use as a guide. Decide who will write the policy and how it will be adopted. This could be an elder, board deacon, board personnel committee, Staff-Parish Relations Committee, church council, administrative council, pastor, or staff committee. It will be helpful to have an attorney and childcare advocate involved.

---

Then I will give them one heart and one way, that they may fear Me forever, for the good of them and their children after them.

—Jeremiah 32:39

---

# Child Protection Policy Guidelines

You can have a combined policy for children and youth, if necessary.

## Definitions

Define what ages are considered children and what ages are considered youth. Define "paid staff person," "adult volunteer," "screened adult volunteer," and "youth helper." Also define child/youth abuse.

**Paid Staff Person.** In the Florida Conference a paid staff person is someone paid by the church and overseen by a Staff-Parish Relations Committee.

**Adult Volunteer.** Specify a minimum age. For example, eighteen or twenty-one. Also specify if a person must be a church member in order to volunteer. Will you allow members and nonmembers to volunteer? If you allow nonmembers, how long should she or he be in attendance before being allowed to volunteer? If she or he is a member, do you require a minimum membership time before one can volunteer?

**Screened Adult Volunteer.** These are volunteers for whom you have checked references and conducted background screenings. It is up to your church to decide if you do national or state background screenings and national sex offender database searches. You will find resources in the back of this manual to help you decide.

**Youth Helper.** These are youth below the age of eighteen assisting with child or youth activities. They can assist with activities but should not be considered adult volunteers and should also be supervised.

**Physical Abuse.** This could be defined as violent non-accidental contact that results in injury. This includes, but is not limited to, striking, biting, or shaking. Injuries include bruises, fractures, cuts, and burns.

**Sexual Abuse.** This could be defined as any form of sexual activity with a child/youth, whether at the church, at home, or any other setting. The abuser may be an adult, an adolescent, or another minor.

**Emotional Abuse.** This could be defined as a pattern of intentional conduct that crushes a child's/youth's spirit or attacks his or her self-worth through rejection, threats, terror, isolation, or belittlement.

---

### Warning!

Background checks are only as good as the police agencies reporting. (Not all jurisdictions are computer literate.) A background check is only one layer of a comprehensive review process.

---

### Screening and Selecting Church Staff and Adult Volunteers

Decide how you will screen adult volunteers. Remember, you must receive a written authorization from the potential staff member or volunteer to run a background screening.

1. Will you do a state screening, a national screening, or both?

2. Please note that not all counties in your state may report abuse cases to the state, so you may also need to do a separate screening for your county.

3. Will you ask for and check references?

4. Will you have the potential volunteer sign a conduct policy?

5. Will you conduct interviews?

6. Will you require drug screening for adult staff, volunteers, or both?

## Ongoing Education of a Person Who Works with Children or Youth, or Both

Decide how often you will require training of staff and volunteers. Training should be required for all paid staff and for adult volunteers who work consistently with children or youth, or both.

Here is a list of training suggestions:

1. Defining and recognizing child abuse

2. Listing church policy and procedures on child abuse and the reasons for having them

3. Maintaining a positive classroom environment, including appropriate discipline and age-level characteristics

4. Outlining appropriate behaviors for teachers and leaders of child/youth events

5. Explaining responsibilities and procedures for reporting abuse

6. Defining appropriate interpersonal boundaries

## Supervising Children and Youth

There are a few general rules you will need to establish along with age-specific rules. Here is a short list of suggested issues for which you should have established policies.

1. Decide what activities will require screened adults.

2. Will you require each classroom used for children to have windows/half doors?

3. Will there be a "two-person rule" (two people supervising in each classroom setting)?

For each age group you should establish rules about supervising classroom activities.

1. Crib/Toddler to Grade 2

- What is the child-to-adult ratio?
- Establish a check-in/checkout procedure.
- Establish diaper changing and bathroom policies.

2. Grades 3–5

- How many screened adults will be required?
- Establish child-to-adult ratios and bathroom policies.
- Establish check-in/checkout procedures.

3. Grades 6–12

- How many screened adults will be required?
- Establish child-to-adult ratios and bathroom policies.
- Establish check-in/checkout procedures.

**Open-Door Policy.** Will parents, volunteers, or church staff be permitted, as reasonably necessary, to visit and observe all programs and classrooms at any time?

**Supervising Non-Classroom Activities.** It should be established that at least two screened adults will be present for all non-classroom activities involving children or youth, or both. Any meeting held in an individual's home should be supervised by at least two adults who are not members of the same family. Any meeting taking place in an individual's home should be approved by the participating child's parent or guardian.

**Counseling Children.** If one-on-one counseling is advised for a child and would be most effective on a one-on-one basis, an appropriate paid church staff person may meet individually with a child.

1. During counseling, having open doors or windows should be the policy.

2. It should also be determined that the counselor is qualified to address the child's needs effectively.

3. Decide if there should be a session limit and when and if referrals should be made to a licensed professional. See pages 20–21 for information on evaluating and recommending local licensed professionals.

**Driving Policies.** Transporting children is an important concern. Their safety can be at risk in a variety of ways. Here are some recommended requirements.

1. Drivers must be known to the designated adult leader.

2. The driver of a church-owned vehicle must be of age in order to be included on the church's insurance policy.

3. A driver must have a valid driver's license.

4. A copy of the driver's license should be on file at the church.

5. A driver and passengers should be required to use seat belts.

6. A driver should be advised of a designated route and should not deviate from it unless there are detours.

7. You or someone on staff should obtain motor vehicle driving records for all drivers.

8. Drivers should be accompanied by at least one other adult.

9. Drivers should receive training for the church-owned vehicle being operated.

10. Drivers should not use cell phones unless communicating with other drivers on the same trip. Texting is never acceptable while driving. Hands-fee cell phone use or pulling the car over are preferable ways to handle talking to other drivers on the same trip. Many states now have laws against cell phone use while driving.

---

### Helpful Hint

Transporting children or youth in non-church-owned vehicles (personal vehicles) should be discouraged, if possible. It is difficult to verify if the vehicle is safe and in proper working order. Volunteer drivers driving their own vehicles sometimes do not want to submit to a Moving Violations Report (MVR). Church insurance policies may not cover personal vehicles. You must check your church's policy.

---

**Participation Covenant.** Will you require a participation covenant to be signed by volunteers or staff, or both? A participation covenant is a statement signed by participants in your ministry (paid or volunteer) that states they have read the rules set forth by the church and will abide by them.

**Responding to Allegations of Child Abuse.** Everyone in the church has a moral responsibility and legal duty to report suspected abuse whenever it comes to their attention, regardless of where abuse takes place. Reporting abuse is a way of ministering to the needs of those crying out for help.

---

### Helpful Hint

Establish a policy for reporting abuse! Check with local authorities and state child protection agencies regarding reporting requirements. Specifically note the requirements in your policy. Cite them specifically, and include child-abuse hotline phone numbers in the policy.

---

### Implementation

Meet with your pastor and decide who will be in charge of implementing the child protection policy. This usually works more efficiently if a committee is assigned this task. Their responsibility will be to design the policy, conduct training on it, and ensure its effectiveness.

# Sample Forms

The next several pages consist of sample forms that may be used as a guide to help you establish your own policies. Many states have different reporting, recording, and screening procedures. Please make sure the forms you use at your church are approved by your church's attorney or appropriate committees.

## Sample Participation Covenant Statement

### Participation Covenant

The congregation of _____ Church is committed to providing a safe and secure environment for all children, youth, and volunteers who participate in ministries and activities sponsored by the church. The following policy statement reflects our congregation's commitment to preserving the church as a holy place of safety and protection for all who would enter, and as a place in which all people can experience the love of God through relationships with others.

No adult who has been convicted of child abuse (either sexual abuse or physical abuse) should work with children or youth in any church-sponsored activity. Emotional abusers should also be barred from working with children. All adults involved with children or youth of our church must have been active participants of the congregation for at least six months before beginning a volunteer assignment. All adults involved with children and youth of our church shall observe the child protection policy at all times.

All adults involved with children and youth of our church shall attend regular training and educational events provided by the church to keep volunteers informed of church policies and laws regarding child abuse.

All adults involved with children and youth of our church shall immediately report to their supervisors any behavior that seems abusive or inappropriate.

Please answer the following question:

Do you agree to observe and abide by all church policies regarding working in ministries with children and youth? ___ Yes ___ No

I have read this participation covenant, and I agree to observe and abide by the policies set forth above.

Signature of applicant: _____

Date: _____

I have read the child protection policies and agree to abide by all policies.

Signature of applicant: _____

Date: _____

Print full name: _____

## Sample Parental Consent and Medical Authorization

Please check with your church's attorney before using this form to make sure it meets the standards set by your state.

**(Church name and address)**

### Parental Consent and Medical Authorization

Name of child/youth: _____

Grade: _____ Age: _____

Address: _____

Apt. #: _____ City: _____ Zip Code:_____

Daytime phone number: _____

Cell phone number(s): _____

As the parent (or legal guardian) of:

_____ ,

(Child's/youth's name)

    I understand that my child/youth will be participating in a number of activities for the calendar year _____, which carry with them a certain degree of risk. Some of the activities are swimming, boating, hiking, camping, field trips, sports, and other activities that the church may offer. I consent for my child to participate in these activities.

    Please indicate any restrictions on your child's/youth's activities:

    _____ I represent that my child/youth is physically fit and has the necessary skills to safely participate in these activities.

    _____ I represent that my child/youth has restrictions on the following particular activities:

    _____ I also understand and give consent for my child to travel to and from these events in transportation provided by volunteer drivers.

## Medical Treatment Authorization

It is my understanding that the church will attempt to notify me in case of a medical emergency involving my child/youth. If the church cannot find me, then I authorize the church to hire a doctor or health-care professional, and I give my permission to the doctor or other health-care professional to provide the medical services he or she may deem necessary. I will pay for any medical expenses so incurred.

I will notify the church if I feel there are any health considerations that would prevent my child's/youth's participation in any of the activities listed above.

Allergies or other health considerations: \_\_\_\_

_____

Insurance company: _____

Policy/Group #: _____

Signature of parent or guardian: _____

Date: _____

## Sample Child/Youth Protection Incident Form

### Child/Youth Protection Incident Report Form

Reason for the report: _____

Date of incident: _____ Time: _____

Place of incident: _____

Name of reporter: _____

Title: _____

Name(s) of child(ren)/youth: _____

Age(s): _____

Briefly describe what happened:

_____

_____

_____

_____

Were there any witnesses? ____ Yes ____ No

If yes, list: _____

_____

What action did you take?

_____

_____

Has the incident been resolved? ____ Yes ____ No

Explain:

_____

_____

_____

Have the following people been notified?

Pastor _____    Bishop's Office _____

Parent _____    Police _____

Deacon/SPRC Chair ____    Sheriff _____

District Supervisor _____

Signature of reporter: _____ Date: _____

Report submitted to: _____

## Sample Emergency Contact

---

### Emergency Contact Information

Pastor(s): _____

Home phone number: _____

Cell phone number(s) _____

Chairperson(s) of SPRC: _____

Home phone number: _____

Cell phone number(s): _____

Director of children's ministries: _____

Home phone number: _____

Cell phone number(s): _____

Director of youth ministries: _____

Home phone number: _____

Cell phone number(s): _____

State or district denomination leader: _____

Church administrator: _____

Home phone number: _____

Cell phone number(s): _____

(any additional contact information for your church's
Personnel Committee, Human Resource Committee, etc.)

City police department: _____

County sheriff's department: _____

State abuse hotline: _____

(You may want to list the contact information for your
state's denominational office.)

Church attorney: _____

---

## Sample Reference Check

---

### Reference Check (by phone or by mail)

Applicant name: _____

Reference name: _____

Phone number: _____

Address: _____ City: _____

Zip Code: _____

What is your relationship to the applicant? _____

How long have you known the applicant? _____

How well do you know the applicant? _____

How would you describe the applicant? _____

_____

How would you describe the applicant's ability to relate to children/youth? _____

_____

_____

_____

How would you describe the applicant's leadership abilities? _____

_____

How would you describe the applicant's ability to relate to adults? _____

_____

How would you feel about having the applicant as a volunteer worker with your child or youth?

_____

_____

---

Do you know of any reason whatsoever that this person should *not* work with children?

_____

If yes, please explain: _____

_____

_____

Do you have any knowledge that the applicant has ever been charged with or convicted of a crime? _____

If so, please describe: _____

_____

Please list the names of other people you feel it would be beneficial for us to contact before making a decision on whether or not the applicant should work with children or youth and please indicate a means of contacting them.

_____

_____

Please list any other comments you would like to make:

_____

_____

Reference inquiry completed by:

_____   _____
                Signature                              Date

You may return this form to _____

(Add church name and specific person to receive reference.)

## Sample Authorization and Request for Criminal Records Check

---

### Authorization and Request for Criminal Records Check

I, _____, HEREBY AUTHORIZE the (*Name of the Church*) to request any local, state, or federal law enforcement department or agency to release information regarding any record of any investigations, charges, or convictions contained in its files, or in any criminal file maintained on me, whether said file is a local, state, or national file, and including but not limited to accusations and convictions for crimes committed, against minors, to the fullest extent permitted by local, state, and federal law. I release any and all law enforcement departments, agencies, and their employees from all liability that may result from any such disclosure made in response to this request. I also give my permission for this information to be shared with those persons who will participate in making decisions with respect to my application.

You are authorized to rely upon a photocopy or faxed copy of this document.

Signature of applicant: _____

Date: _____

Print full name:_____

Print all other names that have been used by applicant (if any):

_____

Date of birth: _____ Place of birth: _____

Social Security number: _____

Driver's license #: _____

State in which the license was issued: _____

License expiration date: _____

Request sent to: _____

Name: _____

Address: _____

Phone number: _____

- You may need to make a photocopy of the applicant's driver's license. Some state background search organizations ask for race and you may not ask one's race on the application form.
- Always keep these documents in a locked file cabinet since they include personal information.
- The form should be shredded when no longer needed.

# Information and Resources for Various Disorders, Diseases, and Disabilities

**Arthritis Foundation**

www.arthritis.org/ja-alliance-main.php

Juvenile arthritis (JA) refers to any form of arthritis or an arthritis-related condition that develops in children or teenagers who are less than eighteen years of age. Approximately 294,000 children under the age of eighteen are affected by pediatric arthritis and rheumatologic conditions.

**Autism Society**

1-800-3AUTISM

www.autism-society.org

The Autism Society increases awareness, acts as an advocate for services, and supplies treatment information, educational material, and research findings.

**Children and Adults with Attention-Deficit/ Hyperactivity Disorder**

www.chadd.org

Children and Adults with Attention-Deficit/ Hyperactivity Disorder (CHADD) provides a support network for parents and caregivers; provides a forum for continuing education; serves to be a community resource and disseminate accurate, evidence-based information about AD/HD to parents, educators, adults, professionals, and the media; promotes ongoing research; and strives to be an advocate on behalf of the AD/HD community.

## First Signs
978-346-4380
www.firstsigns.org

First Signs advocates early identification and treatment intervention of children with developmental disorders. The M-CHAT (modified checklist for autism in toddlers) is available for downloads here: http://www.firstsigns.org/downloads/m-chat.PDF.

## Juvenile Diabetes Research Foundation International
http://www.jdrf.org/

The Juvenile Diabetes Research Foundation International is the leading charitable funder and advocate of type 1 diabetes research worldwide.

## National Dissemination Center for Children with Disabilities
800-695-0285
www.nichcy.org

NICHCY serves as a hub of information on disabilities in children and youth including research-based educational practices, the Individuals with Disabilities Education Act (IDEA), and No Child Left Behind.

## National Down Syndrome Society

1-800-211-4602

www.ndss.org

According to its Web site, "the mission of the National Down Syndrome Society is to be the national advocate for the value, acceptance and inclusion of people with Down syndrome." It offers resources that help people understand, advocate for, and support those with childhood illnesses and learning disabilities.

## Sensory Processing Disorder/Sensory Integration Disorder/Sensory Integration Dysfunction

www.sensory-processing-disorder.com

This Web site helps individuals understand symptoms, diagnoses, treatments, and coping skills for those with Sensory Processing Disorder.

## Tourette Syndrome Association

www.tsa-usa.org

Develops educational information for parents, caregivers, physicians, and agencies. Helps coordinate services for persons with Tourette Syndrome (TS).

## US Autism and Asperger Association (USAAA)

www.usautism.org

USAAA is dedicated to helping individuals on the autism spectrum achieve their fullest potential by providing educational support and solutions.

# Recommended Reading for Children

**Children's Devotional Guide**

*Jesus Calling: 365 Devotions for Kids* (Thomas Nelson, 2010)

**Bibles**

*The NKJV Explorer's Study Bible—Boy's Blue Edition* (Tommy Nelson, 2010)

*The NKJV Explorer's Study Bible—Girl's Purple Edition* (Tommy Nelson, 2010)

*Angel Wings Bible, ICB* [International Children's Bible translation] (Tommy Nelson, 2010)

# Chapter 8

## The First Year in Ministry
### What Veteran Children's Ministers Wish They Had Known

Let no one despise your youth, but be an example to the believers in word, in conduct, in love, in spirit, in faith, in purity.

—1 Timothy 4:12

I e-mailed, sent Facebook messages, and called many colleagues in ministry who have served in ministry for at least five years and told them I was writing a book. I asked them to respond to a simple question: "What do you wish you would have known your first year in ministry that you know now?" I also informed them I would need permission to use each person's name or at least the name of the person's first church, current church, or denomination. It seemed like a simple question and a simple request.

I was surprised by the response. My inbox was full of stories. I received several calls from friends wishing to share their experiences, but not one person wanted his or her name, church, or denomination mentioned. I have to admit this had me quite perplexed and I do not "perplex" easily.

I knew I needed to find a way to share their responses but be respectful of their wishes.

Since one of my favorite theologians is Theodor Geisel (better known as Dr. Seuss), I thought I would share with you the wisdom from anonymous veterans in a creative way.

## The Things You Will Know

'Twas the first year of my first job and I was excited
To survive six interviews and then be invited
To play all day with kids and have fun.
At the end of the month I would receive a large sum
Of money, adoration, or help with my mission.
Then I leaned a bad word in church called *division*.
Not everyone on staff was filled with kindness
and cheer,
I should not have encountered that my first year.
Church should have been happy and perfect each day
As we just prayed and focused on showing people
the way,
To learn about God, Jesus, and the Holy Spirit,
About the wages of sin and not to go near it.
Why were there so many meetings discussing carpet
and paint?
I wanted my pastor to be perfect but found out he's
no saint.
I had trouble focusing on sharing the "good news"
When I had to spend hours discussing placement
of pews.

The computer hated me, the custodian was a pain,
The church secretary kept mispronouncing my name.
My desk chair was broken, my office was a closet,
We did not even have direct deposit.
There was not a Web site or intercom system,
I had to hunt down my coworkers, sit face-to-face,
and listen.
I was told colored paper was way too expensive
And my communication to parents should be
more extensive.
The parents were too busy to teach Sunday school classes
Because the schedule conflicted with their season
sports passes.
I had to recruit volunteers. I could not do it myself.
It helped me to realize even Jesus had twelve.
He didn't have Facebook, text messaging, or Twitter
So I could not think of being a quitter.
The church was not perfect nor was it supposed to be;
It was filled with people exactly like me.
Imperfect people who needed Christ in their hearts,
All finding their way, needing a good start.
So back to the children my focus would go
And back to the God I wanted them to know.


I had to learn the church needed to run like a business
And I had to be responsible with resources to be a
good witness.
Forget church politics and make ministry the focus.
Do not ever tell children about the plague of locusts.

It will keep them up with nightmares all night
And parents will call you and not with delight.
Spend time with adults who are the same age as you
So you will not be using phrases like "number one" and
"number two."
Treat everyone on your staff with respect;
Look for those who feel a sense of neglect.
The custodian and church secretary are as precious
as gold,
Do not ever let this important information go untold.
Keep them informed of what all you have planned.
You will want them and need them to be your fans.
Respect your pastors and surround them in prayer.
Remember God is the one who appointed them there.
Know they have traveled down paths you have not
When it comes to grace they deserve quite a lot.
You will have to give grace in order to receive it,
You will need a lot so you better believe it.
Confidentiality matters! Trust is earned. Don't
misuse it.
It is not always earned back after you lose it.
Don't get caught up in arguments about Scripture
being inerrant,
Don't ever dismiss advice from a parent.
Remember, you are to be spiritually growing,
Living your faith is more important than knowing
All the books of the Bible or the apostles by name.
Don't forget Jesus and the reason He came
To earth to show love and mercy to all.
So there in your closet remember your call.

You are called to serve the least, lost, and last;
The God who called you is aware of your past.
Don't let people use your past to define you,
Remember the cross and let it remind you
You are a new person transformed by the Spirit
Where there is negativity or jealousy, confront it,
don't fear it.
Ministry is a job, no way to deny it,
Rely on God's word and learn to apply it
To every part of your life no matter how small.
Remember the privilege of receiving His call.

# Chapter 9

## The Horrible, No-Good, Very Sad Days of Children's Ministry
### Dealing with Grief and Loss

The LORD *is* good,
A stronghold in the day of trouble;
And He knows those who trust in Him.
—Nahum 1:7

Children deserve to live in a perfect world without pain and heartache. In this perfect world only Bible stories with happy endings would be taught and we would draw pictures of the heroes and heroines of the Bible and cover them with glitter and use glue sticks to attach them to construction paper. We would then celebrate by drinking purple Kool-Aid, and eating goldfish crackers and animal cookies.

Unfortunately, we know the perfect world came to a screeching halt in the first book of the Bible. We now have to teach the stories that follow, the ones that have less-than-perfect endings, with heroes and heroines who have scars from pain and heartache.

If you are in children's ministry you will have some horrible, no-good, very sad days. In fact, just by the fact that you are human, you will have some horrible, no-good, very sad days. You will have scares. You will have heartache. I once heard a minister say she would not trust anyone who did not have a scar. I just might agree with her. It always intrigues me how children love to show me their new "boo-boo." They love to tell me every detail of how the "boo-boo" happened. They are thrilled with the possibility of a Band-Aid even if they are in pain.

They also love to show me their loose teeth. They are not at all shy about opening their mouths wide in front of me to show me the teeth surrounded by blood and saliva and announcing those teeth are ready to come out. Sometimes they even ask me if I would like to remove them. I have to admit, I have the weakest stomach and the strongest heart, but they enter into a heated battle when I am asked to pull a tooth. I appreciate the fact that they trust me enough to place my hand into their mouths and actually rip something from attached roots, but the mere thought of touching blood and saliva is enough to make me downright queasy. Of course, I never let them know how grossed-out I feel when given the invitation. Instead, I remind them how much their parents are looking forward to pulling those teeth and how I would never take that experience away from them. I offer them wet paper towels for comfort and help them to get involved in the current activity. It never fails, within ten minutes they run back and *hand* me their teeth. *Ick!* I compliment them on their great dental skills and immediately wrap those teeth in napkins, place them in ziplock bags, write their names on the bags, and draw huge smiley faces on them. I then save them for their parents. Even as I scrub my hands and follow with hand sanitizer, I see the children are filled with such a sense of accomplishment and excitement. They had teeth that needed to come out. It was painful and messy and now have huge gaps for everyone to see and they are proud of their achievements. They smile as wide as possible to display the new gaps left behind.

I often wonder how we go from those huge smiles displaying empty spaces to hiding our gaps, scars, and boo-boos. When and why do we work so hard to cover each boo-boo, scar, or open gap? We even change our style of Band-Aid. We no longer like our Band-Aids to display superheroes or fun designs. We want them to be the color of our skin so they will blend in and not reveal imperfections. We are embarrassed and ashamed of the gaps left behind when we have had to remove something unhealthy or not needed, or to provide an area for new growth. I do not know the answers to these questions, but I do know at some point in your ministry you will ask yourself similar questions.

The horrible, no good, very sad days in children's ministry can be the hurt or sadness you feel because of something or someone in the church, or hurt and sadness experienced by the children you minister to. Both will happen. You can and will get through them. Some days all you will need is a ziplock bag and a napkin. Other days will require much more. I am willing to show you my gaps and scars because Matthew 18:3 tells me to. When I read that verse it says to me that I must become like a child to enter the kingdom of heaven. I believe it means I need to show my scars, not be afraid of gaps, and share what I have learned.

The first horrible, no good, very bad day in ministry I can remember occurred when I was twenty-three years old and serving my first church. It was my first full-time ministry position. It was more than twenty years ago but I remember it like it was yesterday. It was very late at night. I was sitting on the couch with my husband and two dogs watching a movie, and the phone rang. I answered and the person on the telephone said two words: "She's gone." I knew immediately what she was talking about. Our friend Leah had been diagnosed with leukemia. It had advanced much quicker than anyone expected. She was young, beautiful, kind, funny, and a wonderful mother to three amazing children. She was my friend, and I loved her. I hung up the phone and felt as though someone had kicked me in the stomach. I was heartbroken. I had so many questions, and they all began with "why." I then remembered her children. They were asleep, but I knew they would need me. I had no idea what to say or do. I just knew I needed to go to the house as early as possible the next morning. The remainder of the night I prayed; I cried; and I wrote elaborate monologues and scripts in my head of words I would say to bring comfort.

I arrived at the home before dawn. The house was already filled with people. I entered the door knowing I was completely lost. I had no idea what I was doing. I was young, inexperienced, sad, and extremely nervous. As I walked into the living room I was told all three children were awake and knew their mom had passed away. The father was speaking with the pastor and the three children—ages three, seven, and eleven—were in various parts of the house. The grandmother held the three-year-old tightly, while the little girl played with a doll and held her mom's nightgown like a blanket. The seven-year-old was sitting with his uncles discussing sports cards. It was an awkward scene because the uncles were still in shock and resembled mannequins, and the seven-year-old was moving and jumping around nervously. The eleven-year-old was up in his room alone with the door shut. I decided to begin my visit with the eleven-year-old since he was alone. I walked upstairs, knocked on his door, and told him I was there. He answered, "Okay." I stood a while waiting for the door to open but it did not. Since I was not invited to go inside, I decided I would give him a few minutes. I sat in the hallway and waited.

While I was waiting I could hear noises from downstairs. There were doors opening and closing. There was crying, laughing, the sounds of furniture moving and groceries being stored in containers and cupboards. I could also hear people scurrying about the house searching for important documents. I listened. I prayed. I sat. I waited. I wondered what *I should* be doing. I did not move. A few minutes later I realized I had fallen asleep. I looked at my watch in panic and realized I had slept for only fifteen minutes. *What?* I had fallen asleep. Who comes to a house to minister to someone and falls asleep? It was apparent I was unfit for ministry. I felt unworthy and ill equipped. I had failed my friend Leah. She trusted me to help her children and all I did was show up and sleep in her hallway.

While I was deejaying my own pity party in my head I heard a noise from the door beside me. The doorknob was turning and the eleven-year-old walked out of his room and sat silently beside me. I looked at him and out came my brilliant words of wisdom. I simply said, "I am here." He looked at me, gave a slight smile, and replied, "I know." We sat there without saying a word. We just listened to the noises coming from downstairs. In about an hour we began to smell food. I asked him if he was hungry. He said he was and we went downstairs. He was met with hugs, pats on the back, and was soon surrounded by his extended family and given a large plate of food. I emptied garbage cans, collected used paper plates and cups, rearranged chairs, and organized a pile of shoes beside the door. I knew I needed to be there, but other than walking down the stairs with the eleven-year-old, my ministry to the children was not much more than making an appearance, doing some cleaning tasks, and being a familiar face at the visitation and funeral. Looking back at this experience I now know of many things that should have been done differently. I would love to say that was my last encounter with children needing ministry because of the loss of a parent or sibling, but it was not.

I have learned and grown in my ministry over the years. I have experienced much personal grief in the last fifteen years that has given me great insight to helping others deal with grief. I would have chosen easier avenues of learning, but I do not know if the lessons would have left the same impact if they had not been so personal and painful. If I had not received my own scars, my own open gaps for everyone to see, I might not be as sensitive to the needs of others.

My prayer is that you do not have to experience such difficulties in your personal life or ministry in order to prepare you for horrible, no-good, very sad days in ministry. Instead I would rather this manual provide you with some basic skills, tools, ideas, or Scripture that will help you provide the best possible ministry to families in need.

The first step is to remember everyone experiences and expresses grief in different ways. No two situations will be the same. Prayer and Scripture are essential. God will give you the strength you need. Search God's Word for guidance and comfort.

These verses have helped me.

> In you, O Lord, I put my trust;
> Let me never be ashamed;
> Deliver me in Your
>     righteousness.
> Bow down Your ear to me,
> Deliver me speedily;
> Be my rock of refuge,
> A fortress of defense to save me.
>
> For you *are* my rock and my
>     fortress;
> Therefore, for Your name's sake,
> Lead me and guide me.

> Pull me out of the net which they
>     have secretly laid for me,
> For You *are* my strength.
> Into Your hand I commit my
>     spirit;
> You have redeemed me, O LORD
>     God of truth.

—Psalm 31:1-5

# Reminders and Suggestions to Help Minister to Grieving Families

Remain strong and in control. They need to see you as a minister. You may be devastated, heartbroken, and want to sob hysterically. If so, do it in private. Be strong in front of the family. This does not mean you do not shed tears at times, but remember you have to keep yourself together to provide help.

Talk privately with the parent or parents and explain that the service may be too intense for younger children. Of course, parents want their children near them in the service, whether it is for a parent or a sibling. That is fine and natural. Encourage the parent to tape the service so children can watch it when they are older or on the anniversary of the death. They will be able to understand and appreciate the service more as they become older. It is also a great reminder to them of what their parent or sibling was like. They worry they will forget.

Recommend to a parent that she or he may want to designate a "safe" person for a child to go to if he or she feels overwhelmed during the funeral, memorial service, visitation, or graveside ceremony. It can be a special friend, relative, or you. You may want to provide a bag of age-appropriate activities and snacks to help. The parent may want to grant that person permission to take the child outside the service to walk around if needed. This way the parent is not trying to control or console a child while attending the service and dealing with personal grief. Everyone needs the opportunity to experience and express grief at their own pace in their own way. Some parents will want even their smallest children with them. Of course that is fine. You can still offer a small bag of age-appropriate items to help.

Help the parent understand that children grieve differently. When they see the house is full of family and friends bringing food, it seems like a party. But the sadness expressed by visitors confuses them. They may be unsure how to act. They are happy about seeing family and friends but sad because someone they love is not present and others they love are so sad. I had a parent call me because his eight-year-old son was out playing basketball when his sister had passed away the day before. The father was concerned his son did not love his sister. I explained the reaction from the son was not rare at all. It did not mean he did not love his sister; it just meant he was neither ready to deal nor capable of dealing with his grief at the time. Basketball was his comfort. The father appreciated having someone to talk to and just needed reassurance.

Never enter the home empty-handed. It is always easier to begin conversations with adults or children when you are handing them something. I have a wonderful Jesus doll I like to give to children who are dealing with grief. It is a stuffed doll that is perfect for hugging.* It is probably the most appropriate for children between the ages of three and nine. You may be surprised to know that boys appreciate the doll as much as girls. After all, Jesus really is a hero. Stuffed animals or a small toy truck or car are wonderful for younger children. I once used coloring sheets from a Christian coloring book to wrap the toy. Each page I used was a picture reminder of Jesus caring for others. I was surprised to find that was the child's favorite part of the gift. He sat coloring as we talked about how Jesus was caring for him. Older boys and girls are a little more difficult. Age-appropriate journals and cool pens are appreciated. You can consult with friends or relatives if you need other ideas.

Talk to each child in the family. Do not forget the little ones. You can give hugs, play a game, or ask them to show you their rooms or tell you about their day. They want and need your love and attention. This is true of children of all ages. Engage them in conversation. Ask open-ended questions like, What has your day been like today? How does it feel to have this many people in your house? What do you think is happening? Always invite them to ask you questions. Answer them as honestly

*The Jesus doll can be purchased from Beulah Enterprises: http://www .beulahenterprises.org/.

as possible, keeping in mind their ages and abilities to understand. Let the child or children know you will be at the services and you are there for them. You are praying specifically for them and you are their very own personal minister. Children need to feel they can go to someone with questions or concerns. They see their parent(s) very sad and do not want to add to their sadness.

Keep communication lines open with the parent(s) and grandparents. Introduce yourself to family members. Some people may wonder who you are and why you are there. Do not assume people know who you are.

Offer to help in any way you can. Do children need something for the service? I was once asked by a grieving mom if I would be willing to go purchase three matching ties for her boys. She wanted them all to have matching ties. She said she was embarrassed to ask anyone else because she was not sure why it was so important to her. She just knew it was. I hugged her and told her I completely understood and would be happy to help. She needed something to resemble "order." The grief she was experiencing made her life feel chaotic and out of control. Three matching ties proved a small sign of order. Through all my years of formal education I never received any instructions on the purchasing of ties. I did know through my own experiences that when you are grieving you never feel anything will ever be normal again, and there will never be order or control in your life. You look for a glimpse of it anywhere you can find it.

Send the child a card or note in the mail. They will see many cards coming in the mail and few are addressed to them. Send a card to each child individually letting them know you care for them. Be careful with your words. If you say you will pray for them, then do it. If you say you will call or stop by to check on them, make sure you carry through with your promises. Children who experience loss may have a difficult time with trust. It is important for you to be a positive role model in helping them rebuild their trust in people and God. Be authentic and approachable. (By the way, twenty years after his mother's death, I found the eleven-year-old boy who sat with me in the hallway.) He is now in his thirties with a family of his own. I apologized for not being a better minister to him. He said most of that part of his life was a blur but he always remembered me as "authentic and approachable." My first thought after reading his response was: "There but for the grace of God go I."

## There Is No Such Thing as the Perfect, Horrible, No-Good, Very Bad Day

I would love to be able to say that I always know the perfect words to say and exactly what to do when I enter a home, hospital room, or funeral home to be with a family to help them through a tragic event. Each time I feel my heart break and my stomach fall to my feet. I am humbled by the trust given to me to help children and I always pray for God to speak through me. I still make mistakes. I think of things weeks after that I could have or should have said or done. Just remember to be authentic and approachable.

# Chapter 10

## What's Your Poison?
### Avoiding the Land Mines and
### Pitfalls in Ministry

Therefore let him who thinks he stands take heed lest he fall. No temptation has overtaken you except such as is common to man; but God is faithful, who will not allow you to be tempted beyond what you are able, but with the temptation will also make the way of escape, that you may be able to bear it.
—1 Corinthians 10: 12-13

Chances are, if you see the skull and crossbones image on anything, you know that item is poison. You do not go near it and you certainly would not consume it. There are certain parts of church work that need a skull and crossbones image painted on a sign and posted nearby, so people in ministry would know there is a potential danger. The challenge is knowing whether there is a clear and present danger. There is potential danger. Potential danger does not serve as a warning to all people. I live in Florida. During hurricane season we receive many hurricane watches and warnings. My husband and I are not natives of Florida or any town close to a coast. I grew up in the mountains of North Carolina, and he grew up in Ohio. When we hear the first hint of a hurricane we are glued to the Weather Channel. When our son Alex was four years old he knew the name of our county and how to find it on the Florida map when they were suggesting evacuations. Our car would be packed and our evacuation route planned. We were ready to go. My sister, Cindy, on the other hand, sees hurricane warnings quite differently. She lives near Kitty Hawk, North Carolina, and is married to Bren, a coastal native. The only way they evacuate is if the wind blows them west toward the mountains. We see the potential danger very differently.

Potential danger or potential pitfalls in ministry do not scare most. We often feel since we are in ministry we are above temptation and do not have to worry about it. Anyone who feels he or she is above temptation underestimates the speed at which temptation can travel. It can move faster than the speed of light, out from under one's feet, causing a swift and hard fall. (These two sentences should be typed out and taped to your desk to serve as a constant reminder.)

Consider this chapter a fact-finding mission. Read each part carefully. Chances are, you will see yourself somewhere in these pages. When you do, make a mental sign in your head and heart of a skull and crossbones to help you recognize the danger.

## Money Matters

It is best to have responsible laypeople receive and count money for trips, events, and so forth. Always have two people counting and recording the amount.

One person should never be alone while money is being counted or accepted. The money should be placed in an envelope and sealed. Two people should place their signatures over the sealed part of the envelope. People should always know where to officially place the money (i.e., in a church office safe, with a secretary, or in the bank). It is not a good idea for people to take money home with them. It is important to always consider accountability, and avoid temptation. You should protect yourself as well as your volunteers.

Use church credit cards responsibly. Keep and document receipts. Keep a copy of all receipts turned in. I was once told to place receipts in our treasurer's open mailbox in the church's main office. I placed a pile of receipts there and the treasurer never received them. Since I did not make copies, I spent countless hours on the phone getting copies of each receipt from various merchants. Since the receipts were from an out-of-town trip, it was quite a challenge. You can always get a copy of a receipt but it is much easier to just make copies of them as you obtain them.

---

### Helpful Hint

Make your own copies! It is good to have a backup.

It is also important to be as specific as possible about the items on the receipt. I was once called into the church office to explain why I had purchased personal items on the church credit card. I had no idea what the person was talking about. The administrator showed me the receipt where I had purchased ten pairs of panty hose. I was a youth director at the time and had to explain that we used the panty hose for a game at our summer kick-off. We had a great laugh. I did not mind being asked. It was the person's job to ask, and it was a good reminder of how the church held each staff member accountable. Remember, it is the church administration's job to ask questions. This does not mean they distrust you. Clarification is a good thing. Churches have audits, and clarity is important.

I currently give all receipts to my administrative assistant Martha, and she keeps track of them and reconciles the receipts with the bill each month. She is relentless about asking for receipts, and I love it! She makes sure I label each receipt and is never afraid to question a purchase. We work on this together before it is turned in to the financial office. Every month I am so grateful for her help. We celebrate each month when all receipts are turned in. Keeping, finding, and labeling receipts are not my strengths, so I asked for help. It is not just okay to ask for help, it is imperative!

If you are not sure about making a certain purchase, ask. I learned this the hard way. I had changed churches and was getting to know some of the youth. I had taken four different youth out to lunch over a period of a few months. The previous church where I had served allowed us to take youth out to lunch or pay for a meal if on a church trip. This new church did not allow meals to be charged, and I had no idea of the policy. I just assumed it was okay because it had been allowed at previous churches I had served. I now ask a lot of questions. I am fortunate to be blessed with such a patient church administrator. She is always willing to discuss any budget issue and sends me reminders each month helping me keep within my budget.

### Speaking of Budget . . .

Stay within your designated budget. We have had significant growth in our children's ministry area, but when people are out of work or losing their homes it is not the time to ask for a budget increase. Many other ministry areas are facing significant growth as well. We are a team. We know if the children's ministry goes over its budget, it has to take money from another ministry area. Look for creative ways to save money. Compare different vendor prices. Ask for discounts, especially if you are buying large quantities. Share resources with another church. Several of my friends are children's ministers in other areas. We all chose the same vacation Bible school theme so we could share props, resources, and decorations. Ask for items to be donated or look in church storage for items you can use. I found a huge box of new specimen cups that had been donated. They were perfect for sand art, and they made beautiful Christmas bells at our Christmas craft event. Some people reading this will be very surprised to find out what they had hanging on their Christmas trees last year.

---

### Helpful Hint

Share resources with another church. It will give you the ability to buy supplies and curriculum in bulk. You can ask for discounts if you are buying large quantities.

---

Never accept payments outside of your office or without two people present. It is too easy to put them in a pocket of your clothing or in a purse or book and forget about them. I have had people try to pay me for an event in the middle of the grocery store. I politely say I cannot accept money outside my office and inform them of our operating hours and where the office is located. They are usually happy with the information and understand the rule.

Remember it is the job of the administrator or church treasurer to ask questions about budget issues. It is important not to get defensive. Be willing and prepared to answer questions concerning spending practices, receipts, and so forth. These people can and will be great resources for learning. Respect their position within the church's administrative structure.

Know the policies and procedures for handling money before you begin the job so you are aware of all expectations.

## Your Personal Life

Nothing will ruin a children's ministry faster than gossip about a staff member's personal life.

### Single and in Ministry

Single people need to be careful in their dating practices. It is difficult to say this, but you should not date within the church. Many young people in ministry find church to be the only place to meet people. It is very important *how* you handle dating. It is best not to introduce to the children people you are casually dating. Children can become attached and will feel abandoned if the person you are dating suddenly stops participating in church activities. It is not wise to date one of your volunteers because you will show this person more attention than you realize, and children and parents will notice the difference. This can also create division among your volunteer team. Do not make any relationship official on a social network before you have announced it to your volunteer team and parents. Think of them as your family. They want to hear this information from you.

It is not wise to have overnight guests of the opposite sex, even if they are just friends. This can cause rumors, and much of your time and energy will be spent trying to explain yourself. Yes, it is a different world, and you do have a separate set of standards you must live by whether you think they are fair or not.

Be extremely careful who you share your personal life with. You also may want to be careful about going on blind dates with relatives of people in the congregation. I spent more than a year trying to explain to a very sweet grandmother that I had nothing in common with her grandson. Her grandson felt we had a lot in common and wanted to continue dating. I was just no longer interested in him, and she was very insulted. It created an awkward situation. It is best to try to meet potential dates in a casual setting first before making any commitment to going on a date with him or her.

Keep relationships with the members of your volunteer team professional. If you must meet with a chairperson of a committee who is of the opposite sex, it is best to have another person present. Meet in a public place during the day or in your office with the door open or windows that provide a complete view of your office. Never meet in secret.

## Saying "I Do" Does Not Mean "I Will"

It is easy to assume when you are called into ministry that your spouse feels the same calling. It is important for you to understand your spouse has certain gifts, and should be able to choose where and when she or he wishes to serve in the church. The spouse may not feel that working with children is her or his gift. Do not assume a spouse will just fill in where needed. This can cause resentment and frustration, which will affect your marriage. Remember, the church hired you; it did not hire your spouse.

Be careful not to let ministry consume you. Your family (spouse or spouse with children) needs to know it is your priority. Make time for your family. Here are some helpful ideas to keep your marriage strong.

- Worship together!
- Join a small group or Bible study group with couples who are your age (do not be the leader).
- Establish a date night and let others know that night is devoted to your spouse. Keep it a priority.
- Take your day off. You must take care of yourself and you must contribute to the needs of your home. (This is mentioned several times throughout this manual. That is how important this is.)
- Communicate often about your schedule. Ministry schedules are crazy and change weekly.
- Let the church know your family is a priority. They are learning from your example.

Never make a commitment for your spouse! My husband was a professional drummer and now works with computers. He is also a gifted speaker. I am often asked if he can play in one of our workshop bands, deejay an event, or help with a technical matter. My response is always the same. I recommend the person call or e-mail him and ask. I never make a commitment for him or ask on the behalf of someone else. It is important for him to be contacted by the person who has the request so all details of the commitment can be shared.

If I need someone to help in the nursery, Sunday school, or a large event I ask him if he would like to help. I never assume he should help because we are married.

## The Serpent Can Take the Form of a Keyboard

It is important to recognize the temptation the Internet has to offer. Of course we all know the use of computers and other electronic means of communications are useful tools in providing effective ministry. We must also recognize the unique risk these forms present.

1. Assume all Internet usage on a church computer is monitored. All correspondence and documents are property of the church.

2. Church computers that are set up for guests or program participants to access the Internet should be in high-traffic places and randomly monitored by staff. Controls should be in place to prevent access to inappropriate content.

Do not share too much information about your relationships on any social network. Parents do not want to read your pet names for your spouse or significant other or how they "rock your world." No one will tell you this but trust me, if you choose to let even one parent or one staff member on your friend list you must be careful about what you write and the pictures you display.

If you choose to accept children as friends on any social network or if you text a child or parent at any time always be aware every text should be carefully written. It can be taken out of context and humor and sarcasm can often be misinterpreted. Always assume everything your write or text is visible to everyone.

---

### Helpful Hint

Be careful about what you communicate and how you go about it. Forms of electronic communication are not private. Any e-mail, tweet, Facebook post, or text can be forwarded or misinterpreted.

---

## Not Going Green

It is difficult to look into a box of crayons without being judgmental. Apparently, colors have reputations. Who knew? Perhaps the Crayola Company, because my son now colors with magenta instead of red, and "pine" is the new green. Blue is associated with sadness; someone is referred to as "yellow" if he or she is seen to be cowardly. If someone is "seeing red" then you just want to keep away because that person is angry. I do not know how each of these colors acquired its reputation, but I do know where the color green supposedly found its meaning. Green is associated with envy and jealously. Shakespeare refers to "green-eyed jealousy" or "green-ey'd monster" in *The Merchant of Venice*. It may have been linked to envy and jealousy before the late 1500s, when it was written, but no one knows for sure. Perhaps the color green hired a publicist to help change how green was being viewed because now everyone has forgotten about the stigma of jealousy associated with green, and instead thinks of caring for the environment. Not me! Do not get me wrong. I do all the things we are supposed to do to help the environment, but I do not ever wish to go or plan on going green with envy.

Green to me is a disaster waiting to happen. I see green as the "green-eyed monster." It is a monster with two heads: envy and jealousy.

It can be jealousy of another church or children's minister/director. You will hear of churches with gyms, children's buildings, play areas that look like Disney World, supply closets that are larger than your entire office area, and computer monitoring systems. You may have one room, ten children, and a pack of construction paper and a few glue sticks. It is easy to be jealous and feel your ministry is not as important. You may wonder how to even make ministry happen. You can spend so much time being resentful of what you do not have that you do not consider the blessings you do have.

Our staff was once at a conference at a large church. Most of our staff and leaders were present for the conference. Our group meeting was held in the children's department. My pastor, Reverend David McEntire, walked around looking at the classrooms, offices, and various other rooms. He came back and said I should not leave the room because he did not want me to see the supply room because it might be too much for me to handle. He was kidding of course, but there was a little truth to it. I remember looking at the supply room and hearing heavenly music in my head. It was like the pearly gates opening up. I marveled at all the supplies and how they were divided in such an orderly fashion. I started thinking about all the things I could do with all those resources. Now this is coming from someone who already has a lot of resources.

I have always felt I have been given any materials I have needed or asked for. I was caught off guard by my jealousy. I did not like the feeling. I love where I serve and feel very blessed. I was quickly reminded why I serve where I do when I returned to the room with our church staff and leaders. When I was back with my "family" the resource room did not seem so inviting, and my jealousy quickly changed to appreciation not only for the resources I had to help in my ministry but also for the amazing people I had the privilege to serve with. You must always keep things in perspective and not compare your ministry to any other. If you are sharing the love of Christ with one child, you are making a difference. Do not let the green-eyed monster change that.

## Warning: This Game Is Broken

I recently took my nine-year-old son to an arcade. He quickly went to the claw machine where you guide the claw to the perfect drop spot and take your prize. My son is very good at this game and enjoys winning prizes for his friends with his steady hand. On our most recent trip the sign on the game said, "This game is broken." My son did not even take a second to turn around and try another game.

There is a game we play in ministry that can never be won, but we keep playing anyway. It is called the numbers game. For some reason, whenever we meet another person in our ministry field our first question is, How many children do you work with? We then follow that question with, How many children are in Sunday school, and how many adult helpers do you have? But why are we so obsessed with numbers? I am always tempted to answer, "I have one really great kid who I expect will change the world." Seriously, we are not defined by the number of children who come to our programs. Really, they cannot come by themselves. They have to be driven by adults, but we never mention the adult program that is so outstanding that it has added one hundred children to our ministry. No, we just say, "We have added one hundred children this year." There have been times when I would have been thrilled to say I had one new child come to a Sunday school class over the entire summer. Do not play the numbers game. You cannot win. Do not compare your numbers with another church.

Your job is to provide the best ministry possible in your current church setting. God may be calling you to reach the dozen children you have in your vacation Bible school. Remember Jesus did a lot with twelve in His group, and they did not even have a building or fancy decorations.

## Flexibility Does Not Mean a Lack of Accountability

There are many night meetings and weekend events in ministry. This usually means you have a little flexibility in your daytime schedule. It is easy to take advantage of the flexibility and not have office hours at all. I know this is especially tempting when there are only a few other staff members, your office is in a completely different building, or you feel you have no one to be accountable to or check in with.

It is important to have set office hours each day. People not only need to know how to reach you but when they can see you. If you have a church secretary or administrative assistant, always let this person know where you are and when you plan to return. It places her or him in a difficult position when people call and she or he has no idea where you are and what you are doing. Flexible hours do not mean you do not have to be in your office. Ask for clear expectations of office hours when you are hired. It is also very important to respond to e-mails and phone calls in a timely manner.

## Meet Deadlines!

Remember when you miss a deadline for a newsletter article, bulletin announcement, and so forth that it makes someone else's job more difficult. Be considerate of others and their time constraints as well. Of course there may be times when you cannot meet a certain deadline. When this happens let others know you may be late. You must also be gracious and understand if they cannot wait for your article. They have deadlines as well. If they can take your article, announcement, or other item after the deadline, it is important to thank them. Do not take advantage of someone's kindness.

If you have trouble meeting deadlines there are several ways you can avoid being late. Many phones and computers have reminder systems. Use them. I am not a computer person, but I have a reminder that pops up each week reminding me about articles and deadlines. It has been extremely helpful to me. You can also set aside time each week to set your weekly schedule and review what must be done that week. Checklists are great. My friends and fellow staff members say I am "old school" because I like a written calendar, and I like to write my to-do list in a spiral notebook. It works for me. Find what works best for you.

## Burnout

It is odd for me to talk about burnout to people who are beginning their ministries but this is when it *should* be discussed.

There are healthy habits you can learn in the beginning of your ministry that will affect how you minister for the rest of your life.

1. You must be growing in your faith.

   a. Spend time in prayer.

   b. Participate in a Bible study with your peers. (Do not teach. Participate.)

   c. Worship!

2. Take time to rest.

   a. Take your days off.

   b. Take a vacation.

   c. Do not go into the office on your day off or spend it catching up on your work.

3. Refuel

   a. Attend a conference or retreat each year to help you learn new ideas and approaches to ministry. If this is not financially possible, attend a daytime training event.

   b. Get to know other children's ministers in your area. Meet once a month for lunch. Exchange ideas, concerns, and information. Offer and receive encouragement. Avoid the numbers game. Remember, it is a game you cannot win.

   c. Read books or articles that help keep you excited about ministry.

Ministry is wonderful, and children's ministry is so much fun at times you can forget you are working. This can be bad because you will not even recognize how exhaustion is creeping up on you. Once exhaustion reaches you, resentment is not far behind. First you will be tired, then you will resent all you are doing. You can even become resentful of other people. At this point, apathy joins in, and you are headed for burnout. Many people take this as a sign to change churches when it is really a signal for you to rest, reevaluate how you are doing ministry, and see if you are utilizing the help of other people. You will also be much more sensitive to negative comments and actions from others when you are tired. You may feel hurt, unappreciated, or unneeded. All of the above could have been avoided by rest. This sounds so simple but I have to admit this is one of the most difficult things I deal with.

You may not realize what your poison is now, but at least you will recognize it when it crosses your path. That is the thing about pitfalls and land mines. Once you know they are there, you can prepare yourself for them. At least I hope you can.